Reclaiming the Connections
A Contemporary Spirituality

Kathleen Fischer

Sheed & Ward

Grateful acknowledgment is made for permission to use material that appeared originally in "Mending Broken Connections: A Process Spirituality," Chicago Studies 26 (April 1987), 37-49.

Sheed & Ward™ is a service of National Catholic Reporter Publishing Company, Inc.

Library of Congress Catalog Card Number: 89-61212

ISBN: 1-55612-271-3

Published by: Sheed & Ward
              115 E. Armour Blvd. P.O. Box 419492
              Kansas City, MO 64141-6492

To order, call: (800) 333-7373

Contents

Introduction

Some years ago, when the new rite for the kiss of peace had just been introduced into the Roman Catholic liturgy, I was at Mass with my mother and grandmother in our parish in Salem, Oregon. My grandmother was on my left, and to my right was a middle-aged man whom I had never met. When it came time for the kiss of peace, I turned to my grandmother, gave her a warm embrace and wished her the gift of Christ's peace. Then I turned toward the man on my right. As I approached him, he said loudly, in a voice approaching terror, "Don't touch me!" The scene remains etched in my memory. What I heard in this man's voice was a plea to be left alone with God. He seemed to want to find God apart from other people.

In the past, many of us thought that was possible. Spiritual growth meant deepening our relationship with God. It had very little to do with the world in which we live. This created a compartmentalized life, where spiritual aspects of existence like prayer and worship were to be kept separate from the social, economic, and political.

We now realize that such a split between God and the world is not only false, but dangerous. We do not live in two separate worlds, which each have a claim on our time, but in a single world with many dimensions. God cares deeply for this world. Our spiritual search today must embrace not only our yearning for holiness and intimacy with God, but also our sense that we live in a world which cries out for help. We want to know God better, to learn how to pray, to fill the longing for something more that runs through our lives. But we also seek direction in a world gone awry. We fear that our planet may not survive beyond the twentieth century.

Several streams feed this fear. The first is the threat of nuclear annihilation. We know that we have the power to destroy life on this planet, and that creates a new urgency for the role of the spiritual. We are aware, perhaps as never before, of the human capacity for evil. We have known Auschwitz and Hiroshima; we cannot again turn away from the victims of torture, the seeds of war. Linked with these concerns is the ecological threat. We are finally learning that unless we care for our earth, sky, and seas, we will render them incapable of supporting life.

When I first read Jonathan Schell's *The Fate of the Earth* several years ago, I was especially moved by the book's final pages. In his concluding plea that we take seriously our responsibility for the future of the world, Schell tells us that only when we restore our severed links with all of life will the daily lives of many individuals start to heal. We must connect, Schell says, so that the walls of indifference and coldness that isolate us from others and from past and future generations will melt like snow in spring. When we give the future a chance, the future's gift to us, in turn, will be wholeness and meaning in our present lives.

This longing for wholeness is not only the heart's cry of our age; it is also a major theme in much of contemporary spirituality. The theme finds a variety of expressions; one of these is negative. It is the effort to rid our spiritual lives of dualisms—those categories of thinking and living that split the world into disconnected opposites and make one greater, the other lesser: spirit and body, God and world, contemplation and activity, sacred and secular. Much of our spiritual tradition lived out of these dualisms, especially that split between the material and spiritual which saw the soul as the superior part of us and the body and this world as at best of little importance and at worst as an obstacle to the spiritual quest. As a result of this splitting of body and spirit, spirituality has misunderstood itself at times as being concerned only with the immaterial and not with physical realities such as sexuality, money, work, and human relationships.

Positively expressed, this call for wholeness registers as a concern for interdependence and interconnection. Many different movements are nourishing this spiritual vision, which has been sounded in spiritual writings for several decades now. Teilhard de Chardin gave expression to it when he challenged the sacred/secular split and all of its consequences. The world is transparent to God, he insisted, and *everything* is sacred to those who know how to see. Process theologians tell us that all that exists is related; body and emotion are as important to human existence as mind. Women writers point to the destructive power that dualisms have exercised in our lives, since dualisms give rise to systems of dominance and oppression. Christians deeply sensitive to the ecological and nuclear crises and those who work for justice in the world have come together in a movement for eco-justice, sounding some of the same themes about interaction among all living things on this earth.

What contemporary spirituality challenges us to do is to reclaim the connections. To reclaim is, of course, to recover what has been set aside. But the word has a deeper sense appropriate to the present context. Its root meaning is to cry out against, to rescue from a wrongful state, and so has prophetic connotations. On a personal level, it means struggling to heal the elements in our lives that are torn apart. Our relationships with parents, children, spouse or friends are fragmented and in need of reconciliation. It means integrating experiences from our past with who we are today. On a larger scale, it means repairing rents in the fabric of our world. How will we preserve the earth's capacity to support life, and live together as one human family? Will we allow others to live and enjoy their share of the fruits of the earth? To reclaim is not only to recover but to redeem. The term evokes biblical images of reconciliation, of new creation, of new heaven and new earth. Once we have recognized the connections that unite all of life, we need to open to the graces that will heal their dark and destructive elements. Our world will then begin to mend.

In the chapters that follow I describe a spirituality rooted in this emerging view of the world. I focus on several areas of spirituality where we need to mend broken connections: between individual and community, self and others, humanity and the earth, nation and nation, God and the world, prayer and action, work and holiness, body and spirit, imagination and reason. My goal is to sketch the elements of a contemporary spirituality that unites our yearning for a deeper relationship with God with our concern, and God's, for the future of the world.

1

The Communal Individual

Life on a freeway conveys one image of our time. Consider a typical traffic flow. Most cars have single occupants, each of us isolated and sealed into our tin machines. We move along, just above the speed limit, mesmerized by the traffic and almost automated in our responses. We observe other travelers from a distance, noting the make of their cars, their expressions, their efforts to communicate with us via bumper stickers: "Have you hugged your kid today?" "If you think the system is working, ask someone who isn't." Viewed from an overpass or airplane, this rushing freeway flow seems a stream of disconnected individuals, each plunging headlong toward some separate destination.

Life on the freeway not only reveals aspects of our age, it also conceals certain fundamental truths. Locked into our individual vehicles we can forget our fundamental connections with others and the destiny we share with all other beings on this planet. "You are all one body, members of one another," Paul tells the Corinthians. We like to think he is simply offering us a nice metaphor. The young members of a drug gang, the noisy neighbors across the street, the shabbily dressed man begging near the doorway of the department store—of course Paul wasn't referring to them. Surely we can choose whether or not we want to be related to these people. Most of us are convinced that we exist first as separate, isolated individuals who then form selective relationships with others. We find it hard to recognize the communal web that sustains us all. Nevertheless, in spite of our deep belief in an individualism torn loose from society and culture, we are slowly beginning to acknowledge the interdependence of all human beings. This awareness is a cornerstone of any genuine spiritual vision.

1

An experience I had while commuting home from work one evening last summer made this clear to me again. The summer of 1987 was a time of drought in Seattle, which is normally renowned for its abundant rainfall. One hot Friday evening I had left my work in a nursing home exhausted by a series of crises, feeling burdened by the weight of human suffering. As I walked toward my bus, I found myself silently saying: "Please don't let me come upon anyone who needs help. I don't want to see any more human pain." As soon as I boarded the bus I opened the Friday *Times* and attempted to bury myself in it. But the daily newspaper proved a flimsy barrier against the suffering of others.

At the last stop before the bus pulled onto the freeway express lanes, a man climbed aboard who was flushed and breathing heavily from his effort to catch the bus. I glanced up at him briefly as he settled into the seat across the aisle from mine, and then I went back to reading my paper. Moments later I heard a loud thud and looked up to see this man lying on the floor of the bus, gasping for air. The woman who had been seated next to him was now kneeling at his side, attempting to diagnose his distress. She was soon joined by one after another of the bus passengers who moments before had been silent strangers. While the bus driver phoned ahead for an aide car and hurtled us toward the nearest freeway exit, these passengers came forward with a variety of diagnoses and recommendations: "My car is at the Park and Ride; I'll drive him to an emergency room." "His head should be raised . . . no, it should be lowered." Meanwhile the man filled the bus with his loud labored breathing, pulling us all into its rhythm.

It was finally decided that he was hyperventilating from heat exhaustion; the call then went out for a paper bag to put over his mouth to slow his breathing. I emptied the remains of my lunch onto the seat beside me, and passed forward my brown paper bag. We all watched anxiously for the freeway exit.

At last we arrived at the waiting aide car, and four paramedics climbed aboard the bus. An extra bus was also waiting at the exit and some passengers left our bus to continue their journeys on it. The rest of us were now so involved in this man's struggle that we stayed to witness the efforts of the emergency team. The medics searched for his identification items, then began calling him by name: "Come on now, Frank, slow your breathing. You can do it." At one point their attempt to physically calm his body movements triggered memories of Frank's Vietnam experience, and he suddenly became a soldier on the battlefield again, shouting of enemy fire and trying to break free to run for cover. We watched as the rescue team immediately took up his metaphor and began reassuring him: "The war is over, Frank. You're off the battlefield now."

Finally Frank's breathing slowed and he gradually sat up, exhausted and somewhat dazed. Then he stood up and turned to face those of us left on the bus. He lowered his head, shaking it slightly from side to side, and said: "I'm so sorry, all you people. I'm so sorry." What came to me at that moment was a deep awareness of why Jesus emphasized the spirituality he did, one so centrally focused on our relationships with one another. Interdependence is an inescapable fact of human existence. In his letter to the Corinthians Paul was not merely developing a lovely image; we are literally members of one body.

Relationships as Essential and Internal

To see our interconnectedness in this way demands a major shift in world view. Previous systems of science and philosophy portrayed the world as a collection of atomic and separate particles which were joined together, much as we assemble the parts of a machine. We could choose to relate to others, but such relationships were accidental to our being since we were already whole and complete without them. Community was a second-order reality which we could enter into if we wished. In other words, we would be essentially the same persons whether we married this or that individual, joined one particular church rather than another, worked in a bank or spent a year doing Peace Corps work in Central America. An understanding of the self had developed which was based on separation, not connection and relation, as the mark of the fully adult person. According to this view, we grow up when we finally become independent and can stand on our own two feet; when old age leads to dependence on others, we experience it as a diminishment of self-worth. This understanding of the self, while deeply ingrained in us in the West, is now being challenged. We recognize it as a misunderstanding of who we are. The term individual is not synonymous with person; for to be a person is to be fully related. The purpose of Christian growth and family life is to bring us as individuals to the point where we can enter into relationships of equality, respect and mutuality.

One way to describe this new view of the world and our place in it is to speak of the universe as an ecosystem. Lewis Thomas says in his essays in *The Lives of a Cell* that seen from the distance of the moon, the thing that strikes us most about the earth is that it is alive.[1] We may have reached a similar insight looking out the window of a plane in flight. Clouds move in and out uncovering vast expanses of land. If we had been observing the earth for long periods of geologic time, Thomas says, we would have seen the continents themselves in motion. Perhaps we would have observed Australia as it broke away from Africa and Asia. The word for this pulsing, changing, interconnected world is organism. What scientists tell us is that the earth is a single living organism, a living system. Thomas says he finds it hard to think of the world as an organism; viewed that way, it is too big, too complex, its connections too invisible. He cannot easily imagine on that level. What the universe most resembles, he concludes, is a single cell. There is no such thing as an autonomous, independent, isolated island of a self. Only in this century have we been brought close enough to each other fully to realize that.

Though Thomas prefers the image of the single cell for our experience of the world, some scientists offer us another way of thinking of it, a metaphor that functions on a larger scale. They speak of life as a cosmic dance.[2] This is a vivid metaphor for what physicists call the quantum theory. Quantum physics has taught us that nothing exists in itself, but only in relation to something else which is in turn related to something else, and so on to the furthest reaches of the universe. The universe is in perpetual motion, as it were, a cosmic dance of elementary particles. Science, so often seen as the enemy of religion in the past, is awakening us to a sense of mystery and wonder at the universe. Life is a process, and we are part of that process. In this view humanity is reinserted into the world of nature. Science now focuses on the network of relationships of which we are all a part.

An organic world view shifts our perspective in dramatic ways. In such a world we are *constituted* by our relationships. The self *is* its experiences. As communal individuals we exist first of all in community and then establish a measure of independence within it. Life is a gift or grace from others, not only at birth, but throughout our existence. Our acts of love or hate live on after us and continue to affect the course of personal and community history. Isolated self-identity is an illusion.

Love in such a perspective is not the attempt to connect with others. We do not become related when we love one another. We are already related. What love does is brighten the web of relationships that is already there. Every act of love strengthens the cosmos, and every act of hatred weakens it in some way. Both grace and sin are social as well as personal. We are sometimes aware of these paths of influence in simple ways. I may read the inspirational story of someone who has developed a shelter to house the city's homeless. It lifts my awareness of their plight and moves me to volunteer to work in similar projects. Or, in a different scenario, I leave home after an unpleasant argument with my family and am impatient with another employee who in turn finds it hard to concentrate on his job and work well with others that day.

To say that we are constituted by our relationships is to acknowledge the presence and power of others in our becoming. We are sometimes aware of this in terms of a friend or teacher, whose influence continues to be felt in our lives long after the initial contact. This is another way of expressing the fact that relations are not external, but internal to who we are.[3] They are not accidental, like a change of wardrobe; rather, they actually become a part of us. We experience this most vividly when someone we love dies. We feel that a part of us has died with them. This expresses, I think, the deep loss we feel when a way of living out a relationship, a kind of presence of the person, is gone. Yet the relationship is still very much alive within us. It takes on new qualities, among them the deep grief we experience at the person's absence. The person lives on in us in a different but powerful way, and continues to affect our relationships with others:

whether we fear or trust new relationships, how we come to rely on or turn away from others. Because our relationships become a part of who we are, they interact with the other loves in our lives, affecting those relations and being affected by them in turn. The relations that constitute the self qualify and intensify each other.

What we choose, then, is not *that* we will be related, but *how* we will relate, that is, whether our relationships will be characterized by love or hate, healing or destruction, fear or trust. We do, in fact, rightly refuse actively to live out certain relationships because we sense that the connection is harmful, dangerous, or frankly evil. At other times the healing of relationships becomes a major focus of our spiritual life. The process of healing brings about a change in *how* a relationship exists in my life—as an endless source of sadness, fear, and resentment, or as integrated somehow into the self in a new way. We are led gradually to see that it embodied not only destructive elements, but opportunities for growth and grace as well.

This approach to person and community reflects the New Testament understanding of Jesus' gift of the Spirit. The Spirit is the power which moves us toward renewed relationships. The focus on the meaning of the Spirit has often been individualized in spiritual writing. But the outpouring of the Spirit at Pentecost was not to isolated persons; it was a gift to the gathered community. The Spirit was given not primarily to single believers, but to the body of Christ. The gifts of the Spirit are meant to build up that body. Thus the Spirit's most basic gift is community, the linkage of one believer to another in the body of Christ. God calls a community. We discover the fullness of who we are by virtue of our relationship to that community.

Solitude and Community

Another practical consequence for the spiritual life flows from this view of the person. It helps resolve the gap between solitude and community. This tension between solitude and communion has existed at nearly every stage of the history of spirituality. It appears as the dichotomy between prayer and action, between the mystical and the prophetic, between spirituality and social commitment. In personal lives it leads on the one hand to preoccupation with a narrowly individualistic spirituality which neglects the challenges of social change, and on the other, to commitment to social action unsupported by a life of prayer. Whatever form it takes, the dichotomy weakens the power of both solitude and social commitment, and leaves the individual feeling torn between two competing sets of values.

Thomas Merton believed that genuine contemplation is always a social experience, no matter how solitary it may seem. Contemporary spirituality is diminished, he believed, because we neglect the process leading each of us to become a mystery of solitude *and* communion. Teilhard de Chardin expresses it by saying that we undergo life as much as we undergo death; our selves are given to us far more than they are formed by us.[4]

The Chilean poet Pablo Neruda was especially aware of this sense of life as gift. Neruda was raised in Temuco, a frontier town in southern Chile. One day when as a small boy he was playing in the lot behind his house, he discovered a hole in a fence board. Looking through it he saw a back yard like that of his own house. Suddenly a small hand, of a boy about his own age, appeared and then was quickly gone. The boy had left for him a white toy sheep with faded wool and missing wheels. When Neruda looked through the hole again the boy had disappeared. He never saw him again, but the incident was one of the great lessons of his childhood. It was an exchange of gifts he never forgot. It brought home to him the realization that humanity is one, gave him a sense of the unity of all living things, and widened the boundaries of his being. He saw his poetry as springing from his contacts with human brotherhood and sisterhood, and he offered his art in acknowledgement of the debt. The most important recognition of his poetry came to him, he said, not from his Nobel Prize, but from an unknown coal miner who had heard his poems and thanked him for them.[5]

This communion extends across time as well as across space and encompasses the generations. An experience of a baptismal gift illustrated this for me. Some friends of ours had asked my husband and me to be godparents for their daughter, Katie. The date of her baptism was changed several times in an attempt to bring together several children and parents at one time. It finally occurred on a cold and drizzly Sunday afternoon. Katie heralded her entrance into the Christian community by crying loudly throughout the ceremony, in spite of the best efforts of her parents and godparents to calm her. After the baptism there was a simple celebration with friends and relatives at Katie's home. Katie was presented with several gifts, the final one from her grandmother, now a widow. When Katie's parents opened this last gift they found the grandmother's own 72-year-old silver baptismal cup. Underneath her own name on the cup had been inscribed, "Katie." This simple gesture identified the link between Katie's faith and that of all the generations that had preceded her.

Seen in the context of this communion with others across time and space, solitariness is not so much a question of being alone as it is a description of the fact that as individuals we are not simply determined by our environments, but must deal with our endowments from others in a private and personal manner.[6] Periods of solitariness are essential to the process of our integration. They are the context in which we achieve some unity and individuality, enabling us to make an original contribution in subsequent relating. Life is a rhythm of alternating moments of receiving from others, integrating that into our selfhood, and giving back to others.

Jesus' own prayer, which is a model for ours, reflects this rhythm of solitariness and community. The scriptures tell us that Jesus drew aside at times to pray. The night before he chose twelve disciples he "went out into the hills to pray; and he spent the whole night in prayer to God" (Lk 6:12-13). During his ministry Jesus periodically left the crowds that pressed against him and prayed alone (Lk 9:18). He sometimes went apart with a few disciples (Lk 9:28-36); at other times he took the whole group off in a boat by themselves to a deserted place so that they could renew themselves for their labors (Mk 6:31). This solitary prayer is in the service of Jesus' ministry.

Solitariness always involves a sense of our derivation from and direction toward others. Even in solitary prayer we are not in isolation, but surrounded by a community of family, church, and world. We transcend our environment, but are dependent on it and contribute to it. Every event is, in one sense, either cause or effect for every other event in the universe. True solitude is thus always marked by compassion for others and a reverence for all being. Because we participate in one another, the starvation of an African farmer diminishes each of us. This mutual influence occurs not only on the level of the whole of humanity; the whole of nature participates in us and we in it. We are therefore diminished not only by the death of an African farmer, but by the damage nature sustains from toxic chemicals.

The Chernobyl accident which occurred in April of 1986 concretized this reality for me. In his report for the Worldwatch Institute, Christopher Flavin stated that radioactive materials of potentially health-threatening levels reached more than two thousand kilometers from the plant and to at least twenty countries. In Scotland and Wales several sheep were found to be contaminated and a ban on the sale of sheep was imposed. All fishing was banned in Switzerland's Lake Lugano, after catches showed high levels of radiation. Throughout Europe people dumped tons of cows' milk and destroyed vegetables, berries and fruit found to be contaminated. Millions of honeybees in Poland were killed by the radioactive cloud. Chernobyl is a metaphor for the interdependence of all the elements of an ecosystem.

Jim Forest's biography of Dorothy Day, *Love Is the Measure,* witnesses to the power this conviction of interdependence had in her spirituality. It is revealed in an incident which occurs in September, 1965. Dorothy and nineteen other Catholic women had committed themselves to a ten-day fast in the hope that the Vatican Council, then in its final session, would endorse active non-violence and condemn weapons of mass destruction. Dorothy had fasted before and known nausea, hunger and headaches. This time she experiences a deeper and different suffering. She writes that she had offered her fast for the victims of famine all over the world. It seemed to her that during this fast she had very special pains, a kind she had never known before. They pierced to the marrow of her bones as she lay down at night. In these pains she believed she felt the hunger of the world.[7]

Dealing with Differences

The world view we have been sketching challenges us to make inclusiveness a key dimension of our spirituality. Inclusiveness is a way of integrating differences into a whole, of seeing diversity as enriching rather than threatening. If I am serious about my spiritual life, I need to consider: How do I deal with differences such as black and white, male and female, straight and gay, young and old? Do I turn these differences into competing categories of us and them, superior and inferior? Do I take those qualities that I cannot handle in myself, such as anger and passion, and project them onto other individuals or groups?

We often create categories of insider and outsider; Jesus invited all to be insiders. He called a community in which no one was excluded, inviting the outcasts of society to eat with him. Jesus' vision of the future was open to everyone. He broke down the barriers between Greek and Jew, slave and free, male and female. Jesus' practice of inclusive table fellowship is a key image for envisioning the future. Salvation extends to all.

There is no room for racism or sexism in Christian spirituality. Yet violence toward minorities is increasing. In January of 1988 a report entitled, *They Don't All Wear Sheets,* was published by the National Council of Churches. Compiled by the Center for Democratic Renewal, the study documents the increase of hate violence in the United States. The title refers to one of the study's main conclusions: Sheet-clad members of the Ku Klux Klan are no longer the primary instigators of such racial violence; more and more ordinary people are involved in it. The report chronicles a startling number of incidents of violence—arson, assault, cross-burning, murder, shooting, bombing, and harassment against blacks, Jews, Hispanics, Asians, Arabs, homosexuals, and other minorities. It is a frightening revelation of our inability to live with differences, to relate in love to the other in our midst.

Sexism has similar roots. It is based in part on a dichotomy between independent and relational elements of existence. This dichotomy suggests that no single person can be both fully an individual and fully related. And so individuality is usually assigned to men, relatedness to women. Men are taught that they are, or should be, essentially self-directing and autonomous; women, that they should serve the needs of others, especially husband and children. Women's service is then assigned less cultural value than male self-direction and autonomy.

Contemporary spirituality seeks to replace this dichotomy with a vision of mutuality. Individuality and relatedness are not meant to be divided up between male and female; they are compatible and necessary aspects of any person, and of reality at large, supporting and enhancing one another. At the heart of reality is a mutual rhythm of giving and receiving, the receiving of others for the enrichment of self and the giving of self for the enrichment of others. In *The Strength of the Weak* Dorothee Soelle describes this part of our daily experience as a net of giving and taking.[8] We are challenged to give without calculating what we will get in return and to receive without feeling ashamed or indebted. Through such attitudes and actions we secure this net of mutual exchange. Such a perspective enables women and men to transcend a spirituality that requires unlimited self-sacrifice of women and allows unlimited assertiveness and self-interest to men.

Solidarity and Compassion

It is also in light of this world view that solidarity and compassion have become central dimensions of contemporary spirituality, key virtues of our time. Both acknowledge our interdependence as human beings. We cannot refuse to see the suffering of others, denying our shared humanity and vulnerability. Rather than deny our vulnerability, we must identify with the homeless, the poor, the prisoner, the victims of disaster. Solidarity with others means that we try to understand as fully as possible all the ways our lives are connected with those of others and the impact our actions have on them. A vivid description of such solidarity is found in the diaries of Etty Hillesum, published as *An Interrupted Life*.[9] Etty was a Dutch Jew who died in Auschwitz in 1943 when she was only twenty-nine. Etty records her thoughts and emotions over the course of two years as she watches Nazi domination spread throughout Amsterdam; as she labors in Westerbork, the concentration camp in Holland which served as a way station to Auschwitz; and as Jews are herded aboard suffocating cattle cars for the journey to Auschwitz. In the midst of all this, her story narrates a radical spiritual liberation from a life preoccupied with narrow concerns to a love that is inclusive. As her relationship with God intensifies, so does her compassion and concern for all God's creatures. She learns through suffering, she says, that we must share our love with the whole of creation. Her metaphor for this compassion is a eucharistic one: her body broken like bread and shared with others. She writes that she wants to become the "thinking heart" of the concentration camp where she is confined and where she dies.

Compassion is a key quality for a global community aware of both its interdependencies and its inequalities, and the relationship between the winners and losers in the system. Compassion is also central to Jesus' life and ministry. As Albert Nolan points out in *Jesus Before Christianity*, the remarkable thing about Jesus was that, although he came from the middle class and had no appreciable disadvantages himself, he gravitated to the poor and mixed socially with the outcasts.[10] Why did he do this? The gospels answer in terms of his compassion.

> He was moved with compassion for the crowds
> and healed their sick (Mt 14:14).

> He was moved with compassion because they were
> distressed and dejected like sheep without
> a shepherd (Mt 9:36).

New Testament scholars tell us that compassion is too weak a word for what Jesus felt. It translates a Greek verb that means a movement or impulse that wells up from one's very entrails or heart, the inward parts from which strong emotions arise, gut reactions. Jesus set out to liberate people from every form of suffering and anguish, present and future.

The biblical metaphor for the drying up of compassion is hardness of heart. Hardness of heart blinds us to the pain and suffering of others. It blocks grace and denies God's Spirit. In our struggle for justice we must enter into the pain and anguish of the world in order to feel moved to alleviate it.

Our capacity for compassion is rooted in the imagination. Compassion means embracing the situations and feelings of other persons, taking their hurt into our own person and history. This requires that we enter imaginatively into their lives.

In his autobiographical account, *Revive Us Again*, Jim Wallis shows us how the power of the imagination helped him learn compassion.[11] Describing his experience of growing up white in Detroit, the *Sojourners* editor says that he had no exposure to black people except for an occasional glimpse on a bus or at a Tigers baseball game. In his effort to understand why whites and blacks lived completely divided from one another, why whites were rich and blacks poor, he began to read everything he could get his hands on. *The Autobiography of Malcolm X* became one of the most influential books of his life. It shocked him and left him feeling betrayed and angry at the brutal facts of racism. Even worse, he felt painfully implicated. He had begun to learn how to feel, and was therefore ready to know how to choose.

As Wallis indicates, compassion is not painless. The more global our awareness becomes, the more we carry this pain. When our world and neighborhood expand to include Africa and world hunger, napalmed children and villages destroyed by floods, racism and torture, we can become overwhelmed by the agony of the world at large. That is why compassion can only be sustained if our spirituality also opens us to the grace and power of relationships, those with God as well as with other persons and things which give us life.

Compassion and solidarity flow from a vision of the self in which connection is a central motif. To be a self in this vision is not be be a separate and isolated individual, but rather to be widely and deeply related to the world and other selves, being shaped by them and in turn shaping a world. Compassion is the full expression of a world view in which we understand ourselves to be communal individuals, members of the one body Paul describes to the Corinthians.

Notes

1. *The Lives of a Cell: Notes of a Biology Watcher* (New York: The Viking Press, 1974).

2. See, for example, Fritjof Capra, *The Tao of Physics* (New York: Bantam Books, 1984).

3. Marjorie Suchocki has a helpful discussion of internal relations in "Weaving the World," *Process Studies* 14 (1985), 76-86.

4. *The Divine Milieu* (New York: Harper & Row, 1960), pp. 76-77.

5. Recounted in Lewis Hyde, *The Gift. Imagination and the Erotic Life of Property* (New York: Random House, 1979), pp. 280-282.

6. See Alfred North Whitehead, *Religion in the Making* (New York: World Publishing Co., 1960), p. 86.

7. (Mahwah, New Jersey: Paulist Press, 1986), pp. 154-155.

8. (Philadelphia: Westminster Press, 1984), p. 33.

9. (New York: Simon & Schuster, 1985).

10. (Maryknoll, New York: Orbis Books, 1978), p. 27.

11. (New York: Abingdon Press, 1983).

2

Prayer in a Relational World

When I teach courses on prayer, I find that people often believe that prayer leads them to God but that it at least temporarily pulls them away from any concern for action and other people. No matter what else we might have learned about prayer, we somehow retain an image of it as a kind of private experience that has to be consciously reintegrated with the rest of life, much the way a hiker in the wilderness has to find her way back to civilization again. This sense of prayer as intrinsically isolated from life stems in part from the split we have established between God and the world; seeking the face of God then means turning from the world. It also arises from the fact that the form of prayer that makes our bonds with others most explicit, intercessory prayer, has been relegated to lowest rank. Though it is perhaps the most universal and spontaneous of human prayers, and one of the prominent forms of biblical prayer, we are slightly apologetic about our intercessions, convinced that they are evidence of the elementary state of our prayer life.

Prayer, no matter what its mode, is in fact the path to increased awareness of our oneness with God, with one another and with the world. Prayer does not take us away from action and other people; it takes us to them by uniting us with their ground and center. As the Psalmist says,

I shall walk in the presence of God
in the land of the living (Ps 116:9).

15

When we pray, we no longer see things as cut off from their deeper reality, but as an organic whole. Our ordinary consciousness constantly separates and isolates things. Preoccupation with immediate worries or past problems as well as the scattered nature of our busy lives dulls our awareness of God's presence. Prayer opens us to the ground of love through which all things find their identity and uniqueness.

Even in the most solitary prayer, we remain linked with the whole world. St. Basil expressed this bond between prayer and other people succinctly when, after a trip to the eremitical settlements of the Egyptian desert, he remarked, "That is all very well, but whose feet will they wash?" Rather than isolating us from others, prayer can deepen our sense of relatedness to all creation. In this chapter we will see how this is true both of contemplative and of intercessory prayer.

Contemplation As a Path to Reconciliation

A technological society such as ours is built on the manipulation of the environment. Technology drives us to use things to make other things. So we chop down trees to develop paper and wood products. We learn to create artificial organs and do transplants. Genetic engineering gives us the ability to control life processes. All such activity presupposes a certain kind of stance before reality. We look at a field in terms of what it will produce for human consumption. We approach land as a means of providing human sustenance. As a people we are productive, active, striving for speed and efficiency.

Technology has been able to bring many improvements to human life; it has eliminated diseases and freed us to create works of beauty. These are blessings and true human achievements. But we must be aware of what it does to our attitude toward creation and others. This blindness is apparent, for example, in the actions of multinational corporations in under-developed countries. With a focus on profit rather than people, they often introduce technology which dislocates populations, destroying land and forests, while increasing the country's poverty. Without a glimpse of a purpose and presence that transcends our own and to whose service we are bound, technology can become simply self-indulgent. We fail to see it as a power integrated with nature, and instead view it as a power over nature.

Technology promises a kind of contentment and happiness that it simply cannot deliver. It is a truism to say that affluence has left us with deep unfulfilled longings. In *Morning Light,* his spiritual journal, Jean Sulivan states this truth convincingly.

> Human beings are not looking for just anything but for the absolute, even when they believe they are turning away from it, or when they unknowingly repress it in a search for material things. Every passion is an arrow aimed at the other shore.[1]

Material prosperity and consumption have spawned societies of violence and neurosis, what Jane Wagner in *A Search for Signs of Intelligent Life in the Universe* terms the disease of "affluenza."[2]

There is another stance toward life, frequently thought of as the preserve of monks and mystics, but really essential to all human living. It is the contemplative or receptive mode of encountering the world. Contemplation allows us to take in the world and receive its gifts. We then retain the sense of wonder and awe that belong to true human living. Not all of us will be contemplatives in the sense of withdrawing to monasteries or retreats, but we all need the contemplative dimension in our lives. Jesus was a contemplative in the midst; he was aware of the divine presence in the smell and texture of the fields of ripening wheat, the gathering clouds of a coming storm, the faces of the hemorrhaging woman and the blind man, uplifted in pleas for healing. Contemplation fosters a sense of oneness with all of life. In a talk which he gave in Calcutta a few weeks before he died Thomas Merton speaks of this communion:

> Not that we discover a new unity. We discover an older unity . . . we are already one. But we imagine that we are not. And what we have to recover is our original unity. What we have to be is what we are.[3]

Contemplation is the foundation of ecological sensitivity and the concern for a communal life.

Many spiritual traditions speak of contemplation as an experience of being aware and awake, mindful and attentive. What this language presupposes is that we are in fact always in the presence of God. We are always one with other people and all that is. Contemplation enables us to become *aware* of what is always there. This awareness revolutionizes our existence; it makes us live in the world in a different way, alert to the inner connections of God and creation. We open ourselves to an experience of oneness with God in order to experience more fully the divine in all of life. This is the basis of love of the earth and of others. Such a sense of unity undergirds our efforts to treat all of creation with care.

The root meaning of the word contemplation is to gaze attentively at something. The Carmelite William McNamara describes it as a long, loving look at the real. Contemplation allows us time to see things in their essence, to capture their uniqueness and their gifts. It is a natural next step to treat all creatures with regard and reverence, evidencing respect for that essence we have now seen.

We prepare for the gift of contemplation by cultivating the power of attention. It is this attentive caring that allows us to see each person and the world anew. It rewards us with the gift of wonder. People who seem alien or dangerous change when we take them in attentively. Only then do we see them as individuals and not as strangers. The same is true of nature. Sometimes when we are walking near a lake or stream, we may pause to take in the qualities of water. We let it teach us what it can. Moments like these make it easier to treat water with care, harder to pollute it thoughtlessly.

Contemplation is the attitude of heart required by an interrelated world view. What the contemplative sees is that center of love in which all things find their uniqueness. Out of such an experience we learn to see the face of God in the face of every other human being and all of creation. Even when convinced of its importance, however, we may wonder how we are to keep alive this contemplative attitude.

How Do We Nurture Our Contemplative Lives?

Sometimes we are afraid even of the word contemplation. It seems beyond our powers. Life is busy and complicated enough for most of us and practical worries about job and family take top priority. Contemplation would be nice, perhaps, but who has time or energy to pursue it? Nurturing the contemplative within each of us requires first of all that we believe we are all contemplatives by nature, that it is not something reserved to the privileged few. Next we must believe that it is the only way to heal the alienation and longing our hearts experience.

Once we are convinced of this, there are many paths to contemplation. Formulas and methods are less important than the goal of becoming aware of God's presence in our lives and finding ourselves and all of reality in God. The various exercises are meant to lead us to a point where this awareness of God's presence becomes a dimension of all of life.

It is helpful to think of prayer as listening to God. Since God's Word to us is found in many different places, we can pray in many ways: not just by reading the scriptures, but by walking or sitting in the presence of the beauty and power of nature—the pounding of the ocean against the shore, the abundance of wildflowers as the desert blooms in the spring, the variety of colorful birds we find in our homeland. We contemplate as we lift up the events of our lives—our longing for friendship and healing, the conflicts we experience with family or co-workers, the headlines in the newspaper that trouble or comfort us. We contemplate by reflecting that God is present here with us as we change a baby's diaper, make our way in heavy commuter traffic, or root for our daughter's team at a volleyball game. All of these are ways of being attentive and alert to God's presence, letting it transform our consciousness. From such prayer comes a renewed sense of our dependence on God and our interdependence with one another. It opens out into praise, gratitude, and a quiet movement towards repentance.

God's presence may also be experienced as a kind of absence or darkness, a desert in which we must trust that God is with us even when we have no tangible sense of the divine presence. We listen for God's voice and hear only silence. One young man told me that he believed he had no prayer life because he did not find God in sunsets, trees, and flowers, as others did. He knew only a void within, what he called a deep and dark cave. A breakthrough came in this man's spiritual life when he realized that such emptiness can paradoxically be a kind of fullness, absence can be a form of God's presence. This path has been called the *via negativa* or apophatic way to God; we all walk it at times, and it is the primary path of prayer for many people. It serves as a constant corrective to a too simple identification of human feeling with the reality of God's presence.

Spiritual writers recommend a form of prayer especially suited to this path, the prayer of awareness or centering prayer. Based in the writings of such spiritual classics as *The Cloud of Unknowing* and the works of Thomas Merton, this prayer is a way of simply resting in the presence of God beyond all words, images, or concrete experience. It is an exercise in prayer which has as its goal the contemplative attitude toward all things we have been describing. It attains it by a kind of inner conversion, a transformation of consciousness, where our way of seeing God and all else changes.

The author of the spiritual classic, *The Cloud of Unknowing* suggests an approach to help us simply be, one which puts all things except God under a "cloud of forgetting." Choose a word, preferably one of a single syllable, like "God" or "love."

> But choose one that is meaningful to you. Then fix it in your mind so that it will stay there come what may. This word will be your defense in conflict and in peace. Use it to beat upon the cloud of darkness above you and to subdue all distractions, consigning them to the *cloud of forgetting* beneath you.[4]

Such prayer asks that we simply *be,* letting go of our thoughts, plans, concerns and anxieties. We let ourselves be in faith and love with the Presence within, returning gently to our word whenever other concerns enter our awareness. Some manuals on prayer suggest that we spend twenty minutes in the morning and twenty minutes in the afternoon or evening in this exercise of contemplation. They also offer help in answering specific questions which arise as we try this kind of prayer.[5]

Many people today are discovering the support small groups can provide for their attempts to pray. Some meet weekly or monthly to do centering prayer together. Others have formed small intentional Christian communities, where prayer and action are joined to biblical reflection. This is another way of teaching us that while prayer may sometimes be private, it is not isolated. The support of the community is made more tangible to many when they join prayer groups. Since it is easy to become discourged or give up on prayer, these groups provide the motivation and help necessary for perseverance.

Intercession and Interdependence

Intercessory prayer has always been a prominent part of the human search for God. That is because it is instinctive. It is the type of prayer Jesus talks most about and engages in himself in the gospels. Christians have been convinced that prayer as well as action makes a difference in the continuation and completion of God's work of creation. However, many Christians have a somewhat schizoid view of petitionary prayer. On the one hand, scripture exhorts us to pray for our own and others' needs, and offers numerous examples. On the other hand, theological emphasis on the fact that God knows the future and is unchangeable has undermined the meaningfulness of such prayer. According to much traditional theology, prayer does not really change or influence God's interaction with the world; rather, it brings about a change in the persons who pray, enabling them to view life from the divine perspective.

Individual Christians have responded in various ways to this split between theology and experience. Some have ignored the theology and continued to petition God; others have heeded the theology and have given up petitionary prayer altogether. The questions remain: What does it mean to say that God hears our prayers? Can the prayer of one person really bring about a change in the life of another?

A solution to this dilemma can be found in the contemporary movement of process theology. This is a theological approach that takes seriously our experience of the world as dynamic and relational.[6] A process world view enables us to pray with the intellectual conviction that prayer does in fact matter to God as well as to the person praying and the persons prayed for. It is possible to find meaning in such a world for both the belief that God is all-knowing and the deep conviction at the root of Christian prayer, whether of thanksgiving, praise, or petition, that it really makes a difference somehow even to God that we pray.

In a process world we affect God by what we are, feel and do. This flows from an emphasis on interdependence. God's love is compassionate, taking the world's experience into the divine experience, suffering with its sufferings and rejoicing with its joys. God receives from the world as a free subject the effects of the world's action. God is affected by our sufferings, triumphs, failures, and joys. These events are transformed in the divine freedom and according to the pattern of the divine wisdom are then influential in God's ongoing guidance of the world.

God takes account of human prayers, even though in their initial form they may not be compatible with the breadth of divine purpose and must be transformed in God's love. They open up new possibilities for God's dialogue with creation in its next moment of existence.

An example may help make clear how this is so. I work with an 80-year-old woman, whom I will call Martha, who is confined to a wheel chair and lives in a nursing home in Seattle. Her granddaughter, who is very dear to her, is involved in the peace movement and sometimes takes part in non-violent actions opposing nuclear arms. Martha believes in peace as much as her granddaughter does, but feels helpless to do much about it. She can pray, however. In prayer she unites herself with her granddaughter and others in the peace movement and prays for their strength, safety, and success. In doing so, she brings to conscious awareness our unity in the one body of Christ. As Martha directs herself to her granddaughter's concerns, she becomes part of her granddaughter's particular situation, which is now different than it would be had she not prayed. God responds to her praying, for her prayer changes the world by adding new redemptive possibilities to the current situation. This does not mean that God does not already desire peace. However, in a process world God works with what is, in order to lead the world toward what it can be. Prayer changes the world by adding a new reality to that world; it enriches the total situation with which God can work. Martha's granddaughter and others in the peace movement can receive new and stronger aims or possibilities from God because of her prayers. And so, the world is different because of Martha's prayers.[7]

Let us look at another example of a common experience of intercessory prayer. We love someone who is ill or in a troubling situation—it may be a friend who is dying of cancer, a husband who is out of work, a daughter who is struggling with a major decision. We tell this friend, husband, or daughter: "I'll pray for you." Then we remember them in our personal prayer or we include them in the petitions of a eucharistic celebration. What is happening here? Are we merely comforting them? Or does our praying affect God? Process theology helps us see that such prayer does in fact make a difference to God. While it does not necessarily mean that the person will be cured of cancer, get a job, or be freed from the struggle with problems, it adds a new dimension to the situation. In the ongoing divine relationship to the world, God takes account of and receives our prayers. They are of course transformed in God's life, but they insert new love and strength into the situation of the person we are praying for, and they are received by God and become a real factor in God's ongoing guidance of the world. We have made a difference. Prayer not only changes us; it affects God and those we pray for.

What does process theology say regarding God's knowledge of the future? God knows completely all possibility, and in this sense is all-knowing; but God does not know what any one individual will do. God knows what would be most enriching for an individual if it were chosen; but the individual's free choices cannot be determined or known until they are made. Once made by the individual, they are taken up into God's life and included in the ongoing divine concern for the world. It is therefore possible to say both that God knows human needs, and that one should express these needs to God. God knows all of the relevant possibilities, and is able to deal with any situation which might arise. But God's knowing in advance what concrete possibilities will actually be chosen is impossible, because this would negate the meaning of human freedom.

The process understanding of prayer also preserves God's freedom. Prayer, including prayer of intercession, plays a real role in the history which we are called to create with God. But this does not mean that God fulfills every request in its form of presentation. Faith in prayer has always meant that if God is God, then the divine response will be free and based in God's total view; prayer must undergo transformation and refinement. Belief in prayer does not necessarily mean that our expectations will be met. They will often be denied, challenged, altered, or negated. God's judgment or evaluation of the world takes place at every moment of the experience of the world. Our prayers are received by God with freedom, and in freedom are poured back into the world as expressions of God's and the world's love.

In addition to making a difference to God, intercessory prayer is a means of strengthening human community. Our decisions create a different world for others to interact with. Since in a process view every entity is affected by every other entity in spacetime, sin poisons the whole cosmos, while love enriches that cosmos. Prayers of intercession are expressions of love in a faith context. The profound experience of prayer lives not only in the separate self; intercession is one of the ways of deepening communion with others as well as with God, thus bringing about the reign of God.

Prayer and action are tightly united in this notion of intercessory prayer. Sallie McFague describes such intercession in *Models of God*.

> We ask God, as one would a friend, to be present in the joy of our shared meals and in the sufferings of the strangers; to give us courage and stamina for the work we do together; to forgive us for lack of fidelity to the common vision and lack of trust in divine trustfulness. Finally, we ask God the friend to support, forgive, and comfort us as we struggle together to save our beleaguered planet, our beautiful earth, our blue and green marble

in a universe of silent rock and fire. Just as betrayal is the sin of friendship in which one hands over the friend to the enemy, so intercessory prayer is the rite of friendship in which one hands over the friend to God.[8]

A prayer of intercession, our expression before God of concern for the well-being of others, may take the form of work with abused women or volunteering to help build housing for the homeless. In faith, we give bodily form to our concern for all others in the world.

God is not only the source of order in our world, but also the source of newness. God knows all possibilities. One role of prayer is to open us to these new ways of looking at things. Judged from this viewpoint prayer should enable us to view the world in a fresh way, to see opportunities where we had not noticed them before. Many biblical characters portray this kind of prayer. There is first of all Mary of Nazareth. One thing that characterizes her is the openness to possibility that flows from her readiness to do God's will. As portrayed in the gospel of Luke, for example, she speaks of a God who can make new things happen even in the midst of established customs. Like her ancestress Hannah, Mary prays a prayer of hope in the midst of shadows. Mary's prayer also binds together many of the themes we have explored in this chapter. It rises up out of her own spirit, but a spirit rooted in the past and present experiences of her people, and it expresses her conviction that God cares, as she does, for the future of the community.

Notes

1. Trans. Joseph Cunneen and Patrick Gormally (Mahwah, New Jersey: Paulist Press, 1988), p. 27.

2. (New York: Harper & Row, 1986).

3. *The Asian Journal of Thomas Merton*, ed. Naomi Burton, Brother Patrick Hart, and James Laughlin (New York: New Directions Publishers, 1973), p. 308.

4. *The Cloud of Unknowing and the Book of Privy Counselling*, ed. William Johnston (New York: Doubleday & Co., 1973), p. 56.

5. Two helpful books are M. Basil Pennington, *Centering Prayer. Renewing An Ancient Christian Prayer Form* (New York: Doubleday & Co., 1980); and Thomas Keating,

Open Mind, Open Heart. The Contemplative Dimension of the Gospel (New York: Amity House, 1986).

6. A helpful introduction to this theological perspective is John B. Cobb, Jr. and David Ray Griffin, *Process Theology. An Introductory Exposition* (Philadelphia: The Westminster Press, 1976).

7. For further discussion of this, see Marjorie Suchocki, *God, Christ, Church. A Practical Guide to Process Theology* (New York: Crossroad Publishing Co., 1982), pp. 203-210.

8. (Philadelphia: Fortress Press, 1987), p. 179.

3

Growth in the Spiritual Life

A recent newspaper headline notes that the average American moves eleven times in a lifetime. This mobility is but one expression of the pervasiveness of change in contemporary life. In all spheres we experience movement as the larger reality, within which there are pauses and plateaus. We think we have family life under control, and we learn that our youngest child is having difficultites in school. We are settled in a new job and then find ourselves unexpectedly laid off and in search of other employment. We experience God's presence and comfort and then suddenly it is gone and we feel plunged into darkness and absence. We depend on a long-standing friendship and conflict arises in the relationship.

This realization that our world is a dynamic one, marked at every level by movement and change, has influenced our conception of spirituality. A concern for continuous growth has replaced the search for static perfection that characterized spirituality in previous periods. We no longer envision the spiritual life as a way of drifting in a calm and tranquil sea; rather we realize it is a voyage under ever-changing conditions. What matters is not so much that we arrive at some destination, but how we make the trip. In the past, perfection was equated with the unchanging; we looked forward to a time when we would reach a state of completion. Now the metaphors of journey and pilgrimage mark spiritual discussions; we are aware that there is no completion that does not open out into new growth. Let us examine the difference this perspective makes in three important areas of spirituality: 1) the meaning of spiritual growth; 2) finding the will or purpose of God; and 3) understanding the role of systems, such as marriage, family, and nation, in our spirituality.

The Meaning of Spiritual Growth

When an ocean liner sets out to sea, the choices its crew makes at every stage are guided by the destination they hope to reach. Every journey is governed by its goal. So, too, the decisions we make in our spiritual lives are guided by the ideal we hold out for ourselves. At some level, often without being fully aware of it, we have decided what we think a good or holy person should be like. Perhaps we frame that ideal in terms of love and self-sacrifice, courage and fidelity, or higher stages of prayer. In any case, we constantly measure ourselves against it, telling ourselves that we should be more patient, generous, or prayerful. Ideals of spiritual growth reflect our view of perfection. In the past perfection has been equated with the static and unchanging, with a stable condition untouched by the turmoil of daily existence. Many of us still see perfection as a state at which we will arrive, or where others have arrived, finally free from the unexpected turns and new challenges, the brokenness and incomplete quality of our lives. This concept of perfection undergoes dramatic revision in a spirituality where change and becoming are recognized as more fundamental aspects of existence than the static and unchanging, where to be is *always* to become.

Some spiritualities portray God as interested principally in preserving the laws and rituals of religion in their present form. The worship of God then becomes a matter of defending the status quo. This separates creativity from God and undermines our resistance to evil and our hope for a different future. It alters the spiritual journey in major ways, leading us to remain silent before injustice rather than speak out, to cling to familiar images of God rather than embrace new ones, to hesitate to use our gifts rather than overcome fear and plunge in.

Once we acknowledge the pervasiveness of change, our experience of the spiritual life becomes one of constant outreach toward the new. We are open to growth, but trust in the slow work of grace. Only God knows fully what this new spirit gradually forming within us might be. Opening ourselves to the divine presence enables us to move beyond our given situations and envision possibilities that may be contrary to our surrounding environment. In the midst of hatred and war, we can and must imagine a world of peace and work toward its attainment. In situations of conflict, we can break with patterns of the past and extend forgiveness to those who have harmed us. Within a history of family violence, abuse, and pain, we can choose to stop the cycle of violence, to believe that we are loved and capable of loving others.

In this way spirituality focuses on the dynamic edges and turning points of life. The spiritual life might best be described as an unending conversion experience. Human persons are called to true adventure, together with the risks involved in any quest for love and justice. Within such a spiritual vision, our attention is focused on directions or tendencies rather than on particular actions, since there will always be an unfinished quality to our spiritual lives. This or that individual thought or action—whether I lost my temper today or ignored someone's need—is not nearly as important as are the *patterns* of courage or fearfulness, of openness or closure, that appear in our lives. From such a perspective, the questions I should ask myself are those which reveal the direction I am giving my life: How am I facing the problems that confront me? How am I using my freedom to integrate and transcend my past? The acceptance of life as a process means an appreciation of the open-endedness of both personal and social development. Change is not an enemy; within it can be found God's invitation to fuller human maturity.

Perfection in such a world is modeled on a love that takes risks. Spirituality is a challenge to adventure. The spiritual journey of Thomas Merton was such an adventure. Between his birth in France, his life in the United States before and during his Trappist years, and his death in Bangkok, Merton's life was a search on many levels, always unsettled and unfinished. As a young man he converted dramatically to Catholicism. In the monastic life he broke the mold of his vocation and became a writer. In later years his horizons expanded into social concerns and encounters with Eastern mysticism. As Merton's life illustrates, the experience of time means moving into a future which is really indeterminate; it is not the unfolding of a predetermined story.

In this model of spirituality we are dealing with movement and direction, what is coming to be. There is, then, less fear of mistakes and failures and more concern over reluctance to develop one's potential, on the dangers of contentment with a static position and comfort in the backwater. It is God who enables us to "get unstuck," to see things differently, to dream dreams and imagine the new. It is God who enables us to embrace newness within permanence.

Finding God's Will

Christians look to Jesus' life for the dominant themes of spirituality, and Jesus' life centers on his desire to do God's will.

> My food is to do the will of the One who sent me,
> to accomplish God's work (Jn 4:34).

We also want to carry out God's design for our lives. However, attempts to do God's will give rise to some of the major issues in the spiritual life: How do I know what God's will for me is? How is God's will related to my will? Appeals to God's will have been used to provide divine backing for a wide range of human activities--from acts of love and peacemaking to murder, greed and political ambition.

Many Christians assume that God has a predetermined and detailed plan for our lives, one which has been established for all eternity and which we must now discover and carry out if we are to find happiness and salvation. According to this view, God's will lies outside of and over against us. Clues to it are found in voices other than our own; we look for signs, and sometimes ask external authority to tell us what to do. God's will has little to do with our freedom and personal desires.

The contemporary theological movement called process theology illumines the struggle we experience in making Christian choices. This theology speaks of God's purpose rather than God's will, and its categories enable us to affirm both this divine purpose and human aspirations. To see how this is so, we must take a moment to understand how process thought describes the self's becoming.[1]

According to process thought, the basic reality in this world is a movement of self-realization which continually emerges from previous experience. As a self, I am a subject or center of feeling, weaving together many different stands of relatedness into my identity. I can only become self-aware and self-accepting through all the relationships that co-create me. This personal awareness is a lifelong process, possible only thorough my openness to others and their presence. My goal is to develop self-possession within a profound relationality, to become a self-in-relation. All that I encounter becomes part of the fabric of my being.

Both body and spirit are continuous creations, not given substances or things. The person and the cosmos are and always have been in process of being made; the full meaning of the human person is found not in a complete structure or essence, but in a personal history or process of becoming. Every person thus aims at being someone, at realizing some unification of the self with other things and with the world. How my feelings, thoughts, and physical awareness are shaped depends on the world into which I am born and the way I include it in my becoming.

In this movement toward selfhood, all of the human loves and the divine love play a role, interacting in mysterious ways. Whatever takes hold of my becoming and enters into it is present in some way—the family I grew up with, the friends I have made, the qualities of the country I live in, the ideas I encounter in books and classes, the values I learn to appreciate. Openness to God, as I shape the welter of relationships in my life into a self, enables the self I am creating to approach closer to the beauty God envisages for it.

God's presence in my life can be described as a persuasive lure, a power that operates as love does, by drawing me closer to its object.

Present in this way, God calls creation forward on all levels. Process thought finds that this presence is conveyed in the image of God as the Poet of the World. Just as a poet draws out our response by presenting a compelling vision of reality, so God exercises tender patience in leading us to the divine vision of truth, beauty, and goodness. God's power operates even on levels of life where consciousness is not present, but it is in *human* life that the purposes of God are most deeply augmented or frustrated, since it is in human life that the fullest freedom exists. Humanity has the greatest opportunity to manifest God's presence.

God calls each of us out of lesser patterns of growth and to a greatness we would not ourselves envisage. Like a mirror, God's presence shows each creature its possibilities for greatness. The divine call is toward interest in a wider good, toward a larger self; if we are open to God's purpose in our lives, we should find ourselves moving beyond narrow interests. This is the way the New Testament depicts the reign of God—as a vision of human wholeness for which we are willing to relinquish everything—our possessions, our security, even our view of ourselves as holy.

God's power operates in each person's life through a stream of conditions and events, processes and powers, which we only vaguely attend to on a conscious level. Sometimes we become aware how the sudden death of a friend, the chance comment of an acquaintance, or a story that appears in the news enlarges the scope of our love and our life's direction. But the divine purposes are largely hidden from view. Since this touch of God comes at the deepest levels of who we are, centering prayer which takes us into our inner selves can be an important part of seeking to know God's will.

Within such an understanding of God's will, the specifics of following God flow from my deepest longings, my relationships, my health and financial situation, my previous commitments, and the political and cultural context in which I live. God's call is always historically incarnate; it is addressed to the actual situation in which I find myself.

Though we sometimes get stuck trying to know whether God wants us, for example, to work with the handicapped or to work for the homeless, to write or to teach, there is needless anxiety here. God has not decided these things for us. They are matters of our choice; God merely wants us to seek the good. Finding God's will is not a matter of discovering a previously determined plan; it is rather a process of making the best creative choice we can make within our circumstances.

For example, a young woman is struggling to know what career choice would be in keeping with God's wishes for her. She is a shy and quiet person, generally uncomfortable with her adult relationships. On the other hand, she comes alive in the presence of children and can never remember a time when she has not loved being around them. When it is suggested to her that she make these part of her prayer and decision-making, she comes to a peaceful and joyous choice of a career teaching young children, convinced that this is both something that will lead to happiness and something fully in keeping with God's purpose for her. The confidence and improved image of self that come from this work gradually enable her to begin the process of healing her adult relationships with family and friends.

What spiritual growth does is expand the range and depth of my love and my capacity for relationships. It enables me to retain my integrity while incorporating greater contrasts into my life. I can experience and encourage diversity and uniqueness in others without feeling defensive and insecure. In this spiritual vision, I can rejoice when others succeed, seeing their success not as my diminishment but as an enrichment both of me and of the web of existence which sustains us both.

In a world view where reciprocity and mutual responsibility are the norm, becoming adult takes on new meaning. No longer is it equated, as it so often has been in our society, with becoming an independent and solitary individual. Rather, adulthood now requires that we reject both dependence and independence and embrace interdependence. To grow in maturity is to relate more fully with all of life. Interdependence is not something to be feared, but an experience we all share as we mutually give and receive from one another.

Discernment of God's will requires careful attending to the reality of our lives as they change and develop. God's purpose is revealed only gradually, since it is a direction and not a final plan. It takes into account all of my responses along the way, responses which influence God's succeeding call for me.

Although we cannot know with certainty that a particular action is God's will, there are criteria for evaluating our Christian choices. As the New Testament authors stress repeatedly, we know that we are dwelling in God's love if we live according to the pattern of Jesus' life, since he is "the image of the invisible God, the first-born of creation" (Col 1:15). Christ gives concrete expression to the ideal toward which God is calling creation. Jesus is described as the path or door that leads to the deeper realities; he reveals the goal of the process of becoming, what it means at the most fundamental level to live in terms of who God is and what humanity is. In Jesus we see how we are to view every situation in terms of God's vision of beauty and truth. We know our humanity in looking forward to the new creation we are to become in view of the possibilities released into the world in the event of Jesus Christ. The vision of Jesus makes people whole, healthy, and strong. Jesus restores people's humanity and life.

The Christian tradition has offered another criterion for evaluating Christian decisions. As expressed by Ignatius of Loyola, confirmation of a choice comes in the form of God's peace, a deep sense of rightness about our choice. Process thinkers would emphasize certain qualities of this peace. Since it results from the experience of God, the peace that accompanies a decision should not only calm turbulence and preserve the sources of our energy; it also bears a quality of movement and expansiveness. We sense that in our decisions we have not escaped life's risks, but rather have found in God the will and power to meet them. In addition, the experience of peace should open us to the larger community, to wider sympathies. Our choices are judged, then, by the way they have enlarged our powers and led to growth in the love of humanity as such. In making choices we are able to remain open to God's purpose while at the same time taking seriously our own aspirations and freedom. This is so because God's purpose is the fullness of both the individual's and the world's potential. It is the divine Poet's vision of truth, beauty and goodness.

The biblical understanding of sin fits well with this view of Christian growth. In the story of Adam and Eve the entry of sin into the world is portrayed as a breakdown of relationships—of human persons with God, with one another and with nature. This rupture of relatedness finally culminates in the murder of brother by brother in the account of Cain and Abel. Sin, then, is our refusal to honor the circles of interdependence that support life. It is a refusal to relate. This happens, for example, in our oppression of others because of gender, race, or class; in our destruction of the ecosphere, and in our movement toward nuclear disaster. Redemption, in contrast, is described as reconciliation, as New Creation. Healing is the attempt to restore the nature of relationships to the way they ought to be lived.

This interpretation of sin acknowledges the solidarity of human existence. Our choices have consequences for others and ultimately for the whole social fabric. We ourselves are affected by the tragic situation human beings have created through accumulated decisions. In our decade we are perhaps most aware of this in terms of the cycles of violence perpetuated in our families and communities, where those who have been victims of violence and abuse go on to damage others. Human solidarity has created a state where the selection of the true good is often very difficult; there is a deep tendency to select apparent goods which do not satisfy the human yearning for happiness and wholeness. This social nature of both sin and grace underlies the importance of systems in our spiritual lives, the final topic we will explore in this chapter.

The Role of Systems in Our Spirituality

The recognition of systems is an outgrowth of an interdependent world view. We exist and choose as parts of those broader networks of persons to which we belong: marriages, families, churches, political establishments, economies, institutions of all kinds. A system is like a mobile;

when one part of it is touched, all parts are moved. In a system the parts necessarily become changed by their mutual association; systems are dynamically interacting parts. Thus they have a profound influence on the lives and decisions of their members.

Because a system has an identity larger than the individuals that comprise it, we speak of a sinful system or, in turn, of a system mediating grace to us. Perhaps this can be best understood by beginning with a small system, a friendship or marriage. Friendships and marriages have an identity that goes beyond the individual personalities of the two persons involved. The current focus on co-dependence has helped us understand how this is so. In a healthy friendship the actions of the two persons support self-esteem and creativity in one another. In Christian terms, we speak of their being grace for one another. In a co-dependent marriage the two share the same sickness. An alcoholic individual, for example, is not the only one who suffers from the disease of alcoholism; the whole marriage suffers from it. In interpreting a friendship or marriage in this way, we look not only at its individual members, probing for the sources of health or illness within them. Rather, we focus on their patterns of interactions. How do they express affection and anger? How do they get their needs met and respond to the needs of the other?

Likewise in speaking of a family that is dysfunctional for any reason, we are referring not just to the individuals in that family, but to the family dynamics. A family may consist of husband, wife, and children—the traditional nuclear family—or it may be composed of a broader range of relatives, of people supporting one another who are not blood relatives, of single parents raising children. Whatever its constellation, a family is also a system, and all of its members exercise mutual influence on the spirituality of each member. This influence continues long after they stop living together physically. This means that many of our gifts and strengths comes from our families, as well as many of the problems we are attempting to solve and the limitations we are trying to overcome.

This insight into family systems is a way of recognizing the power which the past has over our present. It continues to be the matrix for present choices. One spiritual task is finding new possibilities in the givenness of this past. We need to open to God in our lives as source of newness and healing.

Systems touch our lives on an even larger level and have become an urgent concern for contemporary spirituality. We live not only within marriages and families; we also belong to churches, cities, and nations. In addition there are political and economic networks to which we contribute and which influence our lives. Just as sin and grace are embedded in our family systems, so are they mediated by these other systems. It is not enough, then, for me to be concerned with my own prayer life and personal path to virtue. I cannot say that I love God and my neighbor if I remain indifferent to the structures that determine people's lives. I must direct my attention and energy to the redemption of these systems. Since this work is tough to tackle alone, I need the support of others in this effort. Together we need to analyze structural dynamics and develop strategies for action.[2]

We cannot direct our energies to all systems at once. There is hope, however, in the knowledge that they are themselves interconnected. In our time anti-hunger activists and peace and justice advocates are increasingly aware of the interlocking nature of war and hunger. We are recognizing the common ground of all oppression. This means we need only enter at some point in the movement, and our efforts will link with those of others to strengthen their momentum. When presented with the evil of human systems, it is possible to despair. Systems resist change. Only a deep conviction that grace as well as sin can touch them, will sustain our efforts. Concern with systems is one of the ways we recognize our power to hurt and heal each other. The life in the midst of death, which is the gospel promise, arises within these connections.

The more fully we enter into the struggle to transform structures and systems, the more deeply do we realize what it means to view the spiritual life in terms of growth and change. We continue to hope, though our hopes are never fully realized. We search for direction in situations that are ambiguous and conflict-ridden. We celebrate incomplete victories and partial successes. We learn, as Alfred North Whitehead has said, that the worship of God is not a rule of safety. It is, rather, an adventure of the spirit.[3]

Notes

1. My summary is based on Alfred North Whitehead, *Process and Reality* (New York: The Macmillan Co., 1978), and *Religion in the Making* (New York: World Publishing Co., 1960).

2. For help in analyzing systems, see Joe Holland and Peter Henriot, S.J., *Social Analysis. Linking Faith and Justice* (Washington, DC: The Center of Concern, 1983).

3. *Science in the Modern World* (New York: The Macmillan Co., 1967), p. 192.

4

Caring For the Earth

Last September a friend and I spent a day hiking a trail up Mount Rainier, one of the major mountain peaks in the Northwest Cascade range. It was a bright, clear day, perfect for a hike, bringing many climbers of all ages to the trail. A spirit of reverence and play in the presence of nature prevailed among the hikers and their families. People mirrored the relaxed, friendly mood of the natural surroundings—greeting strangers, smiling readily, giving occasional help to a hiker. One group paused to talk with a marmot and squirrel. Further on a mother instructed her two sons about the importance of staying on the marked trails so as not to step on any wildflowers or damage the fragile meadows. Climbers paused to contemplate the distant mountain peaks; children played in the few mounds of snow that had survived the summer sun. As one man approached the face of the mountain, he spoke of communing with it, befriending it. It seemed a good way to express the experience of well-being and harmony felt by those on the trail.

As we reached the end of our climb near Panorama Point, it was evident that not all climbers share the reverence for nature we found among those on the trail that day. Large park crews were engaged in expensive and painstaking repairs necessitated by people creating switchbacks off the marked trails. Their carelessness had destroyed the meadows, paving the way for erosion and the disappearance of the trails. Others now worked inch by inch to save the mountainside.

Our experiences on the trail that autumn day highlight concerns about humanity's relationship with nature on a larger scale. The life of our planet is seriously threatened. Acid rain is poisoning thousands of lakes in Canada and the United States; fifteen hundred lakes in southern Norway are now acidified and seventy percent no longer support fish. Lush rainforests in tropical regions are razed at an alarming rate. The Amazon region is experiencing the most devastating levels of this tropical deforestation, deforestation that results in the dramatic extinction of plant and insect species. Chlorofluorocarbons released by aerosol spray cans and refrigeration equipment, as well as nitrous oxide emissions from the use of nitrogen fertilizers, are depleting the ozone layer in the upper atmosphere. This ozone protects the earth from the damaging effects of ultraviolet light on plants, animals, ecosystems, and humans, in whom it causes skin cancer. With alarm, we recognize the danger we human beings pose to all of creation.

Reversing these destructive trends requires a radical shift in our spiritual vision. Spirituality embraces not just our relationship with God and other persons, but with all of nature as well. Convictions that set us over against nature need to be converted to a spirituality of ecological interdependence.

Several obstacles stand in the way of such a conversion. One of these is the separation of the spiritual and the material, a dualism which regards the things of this world as of little importance. This belief infuses much spirituality. It is found in many of our prayers and hymns, which express the conviction that we have here no lasting home. The material, the earth and the body, will pass away and be destroyed; only the spiritual or the soul will survive. Why care for an earth that is passing away?

Like body and spirit, history and nature have also been separated from one another. Human events have assumed center stage, though played out against the backdrop of nature. This is a distorted picture of reality; nature and human history are themselves intertwined. Just one example of this is the way whole movements of peoples have resulted from shifts in land formations and climate changes. There is fear that if warming of the earth's temperatures occurs because of increased amounts of carbon dioxide in the air, such a temperature rise would eventually melt the Antarctic and Greenland icecaps. The gradual rise in sea level which would result could engulf many coastal cities around the globe.

This split between the spiritual and the material and between human history and nature appears in some interpretations of the Second Coming. Christians influenced by such approaches believe that we must expect the world to get worse before God ushers in the final reign. Events such as the depletion of the earth's resources and the destruction of the world's ecological balance merely indicate that Christ's coming is at hand. In this view, attempts to preserve the earth are pointless.

But care of the earth is not pointless; it is in fact an integral aspect of any holistic spirituality. In this chapter we will look at some resources for reversing the attitudes that are endangering our planet: 1) a biblical understanding of creation that supports care of the earth; 2) positive ways of imaging our relationship with nature; 3) the role of prayer in ecological awareness; and 4) guidelines for moving from awareness to action.

The Bible and Our Relationship with Nature

The Bible does not answer all the questions raised by our new situation. However, certain biblical passages have strongly influenced the human approach to nature. The biblical injunction to subdue the earth seems to support an imperialistic stance toward the material world. After recounting the creation of woman and man, the Genesis creation account continues:

> God blessed them, saying to them, "Be fruitful and multiply, fill the earth and conquer it. Be masters of the sea, the birds of heaven and all living animals on the earth" (Gen 1:28).

Interpretations of this passage have been used to support an attitude that reduces the nonhuman to a means to human ends. Influenced by its message, we speak of conquering a mountain or space, mastering the land, dominating nature. Behind this language is a hierarchical interpretation of the Genesis creation account. Creation is conceived in the image of a ladder or pyramid. God is at the top, and beneath God are men. Next in the hierarchy are women and children, and beneath them are animals, plants, and the inanimate parts of creation. Just as God is to rule over man, so man is to rule over woman. The same interpretation that justifies the subordinate role of women sanctions humanity's efforts to subjugate nature.[1]

Such a reading of Genesis is not in keeping with the fullness of the biblical message. Human beings do have unique value and worth, but other species on the planet also have intrinsic worth. The Psalmist proclaims:

> God, what variety you have created,
> arranging everything so wisely!
> Earth is completely full of things you have made:
>
> among them vast expanse of ocean,
> teeming with countless creatures,
> creatures large and small (Ps 104:24-25).

Creation's importance does not lie simply in its support for human life; Genesis describes God as pronouncing the creation good before human life is even created. Moreover, the creation accounts find their meaning within an understanding of God's covenant. Our relationship with nature must therefore be seasoned by that covenant perspective. God makes a covenant not only with people, but with all of creation. This becomes clear in Genesis 8 and 9 which tell the story of Noah and the flood. The agreement with Noah and his descendants is described as a covenant between God and the rest of living things.

> God said, "Here is the sign of the covenant I make between myself and you and every living creature with you for all generations: I set my bow in the clouds and it shall be a sign of the covenant between me and the earth. When I gather the clouds over the earth and the bow appears in the clouds, I will recall the covenant between myself and you and every living creature of every kind" (Gen 9:12-15).

In this new world order, symbolized by the promise of the rainbow, the unity of all of creation will be restored. The prophet Hosea makes this clear.

> Then I will make a covenant on behalf of Israel with the wild beasts, the birds of the air, and things that creep on the earth, and I will break bow and sword and weapon of war and sweep them off the earth, so that all living creatures may lie down without fear (2:20).

The prophet's pleas for justice are linked to the restoration of humanity's broken relationship with creation. The covenant calls for a situation in which all creatures live together in mutual respect. The fracturing of these relationships is evidence of the presence of sin in the world.

Moving from the Hebrew scriptures to the New Testament, we find similar testimony to the importance of the earth. The redemption accomplished in Christ is not limited to the individual person, but extends to the whole creation. Just as sin destroys this harmonious relationship between God, humanity, and creation, so Christ's reconciliation reaches all the earth. If we think of humanity as separate from creation, we are tempted to assume that we can be saved while creation is destroyed, viewing the material world like a shell that is discarded when a transformed existence begins. This is not the Christian vision. Redemption is the promise that creation, as well as humanity, will be made whole and new. Such an understanding of creation is expressed, for example, in Romans.

> Indeed the whole creation eagerly awaits the revelation of the children of God . . . . Yes, we know that all creation groans and is in agony even until now (8:19, 22).

Reconciliation, in its biblical meaning, situates every creature in community with every other. We are set free in our relationship to the material world. Nature is now no longer an object, but a companion. Sharing in Christ's work of redemption calls us to work not just for the salvation of humanity; it involves a mission of earthkeeping.

New Images of Our Relationship with the Earth

Once we are convinced that faith calls us to responsible care for our planet earth, a practical question arises. How can we bring about the change of heart necessary for such stewardship? Since change begins in our capacity to imagine in new ways, our starting point must be the way we envision our relationship with the earth. We must abandon the vision of creation as a pyramid or ladder of being. Many of us are scarcely aware of the way this picture of the world influences our tendency to treat nature as subservient. Those who do recognize the image's power have begun to propose alternate metaphors as reflecting more fully our redeemed relationship to creation.[2]

Three of the most helpful of these metaphors portray human persons as stewards of creation, as friends of the earth, and as tenders of the garden of creation. We are stewards, not in a domineering sense, but as responsible caretakers answerable to God, like the several stewards in the biblical parables who have treasures entrusted to their care. The second image, friends of the earth, is a redemptive metaphor for our relation to nature because friendship expresses a mutual relationship of caring and reverence. Imaged in this way, our interventions in nature are to be based not on a model of competition and conquest, but on one of cooperation and mutual dependence. The metaphor of tending a garden is meant to stand in contrast with interpretations of Genesis that sanction human exploitation of nature. Rather, the earth is a garden that must be carefully nurtured. The pollution of the air and the water, the destruction of forests, the turning of grasslands into deserts diminish us as well as all other beings on the earth. A well-tended garden becomes a sustaining environment for all forms of life.

Other spiritual traditions can contribute to this effort to envision our relationship with the earth in a new way. Native American spirituality is an especially helpful source of insight into the interconnectedness of all of life. Native American peoples speak not of the ladder or pyramid of being, but of the sacred hoop and the circle. In John G. Neihardt's *Black Elk Speaks,* a Native American holy man recounts a vision in which he sees that the sacred hoop of his own people appears as one of many hoops that make up a larger circle. The circle is as wide as daylight and starlight. In its center grows a mighty flowering tree which shelters all the children of one mother and one father.[3]

In a similar vein, the Laguna Pueblo/Sioux Indian writer Paula Gunn Allen tells in *The Sacred Hoop* how when she was small her mother taught her that all animals, insects, and plants are to be treated with respect.[4] Life is a circle, her mother would say, in which everything has its place. Gunn learned to look to the wind and sky, the trees and rocks, the sticks and stars, to teach her. These attitudes led to a sense of connection to the land and all her creatures, as well as to carefulness in the use of the earth's resources. I encountered this same spirit several years ago while visiting with some Colville Indian medicine women on their reservation in Eastern Washington. Children at the reservation's school had been preparing for a spring festival, and the women had been asked to show them how to find native roots in the wooded areas bordering the school. After the experience the women lamented to me that the children had been so careless about dropping the roots and trampling them under foot. "They will never *learn* the Indian ways," they said, "unless they *learn* never to waste anything."

Through the image of the sacred hoop and the circle, Native Americans capture the notion of a unity that is dynamic and encompassing. Thinking in a circular way stands in contrast to the linear hierarchies that have influenced most reflections on our relationship with nature. All creatures are relatives, brothers and sisters, necessary parts of a balanced and living whole. It is not that nature exists for the welfare of the human race; we are all part of the one creation and exist for the All Spirit. The Great Mystery is at the center of the circle of life, the source of all that is. Everything begins and ends in God; the hoop is complete in God for whom all things exist. Because we are all in relationship with the Great Mystery, we are all in relationship with one another. Native Americans rightly speak of Mother Earth; the earth nourishes and sustains life. It cradles our existence.

In contrast to a culture that fosters detached individualism, Native American peoples stress that relationships among all the beings of the universe must be fulfilled; in this way each individual life also reaches its fullness. An old Keres Indian song says:

> I add my breath to your breath
> That our days may be long on the Earth
> That the days of our people may be long
> That we may be one person
> That we may finish our roads together
> May our mother bless you with life
> May our Life Paths be fulfilled.[5]

Since breath is life, the intermingling of breaths is the purpose of life.

The city of Seattle derives its name from an Indian chief who provides one of the most moving historical witnesses to this relationship with the earth. In the mid-nineteenth century white settlers near Puget Sound attempted to sign a treaty with a group of Indian tribes whose land they had taken. Chief Sealth, whose name the white settlers spelled "Seattle," had originally welcomed the white settlers and accepted their God. In 1854, pained by the destruction they were inflicting on his people and land, Chief Sealth pleaded with the white people to reverse this exploitation of land, buffalo, and nature. The earth does not belong to us, he said; rather, we belong to the earth. We are a strand in the web of life, and what we do to the web we do to ourselves. The earth is precious to God, he insisted, and to harm the earth is to show contempt for God. Chief Sealth's words were ignored, however, as the U.S. Cavalry swept across the West, trampling nature and killing those who loved it.

Prayer and Ecological Sensitivity

Care of the earth must be rooted in the sort of prayer that prepares us for nature's revelations and opens us to the presence of God in the physical world. Teilhard de Chardin pointed the way into such prayer when he spoke of the world as the outward and visible presence of God. Opening to this presence means learning again how to see, how to contemplate the world. A mystic awareness of God's presence in creation is the foundation of responsible planning. Teilhard articulated this vision in his "Mass on the World."[6] While on a scientific expedition he found himself one day in the Ordos desert without the chalice or the bread and wine he needed to offer Mass. It was the feast of the Transfiguration, and Teilhard's thoughts turned to the divine presence throughout the universe. Teilhard made the whole earth his altar, and lifted up as his offering, the whole of creation. As a paleontologist, Teilhard's spirituality was cosmic in scope. He saw the history of the cosmos in terms of billions of years; human life appeared on the scene only a few million years ago. Our present conditions of life are even more recent.

While Teilhard taught us to see creation from the perspective of time, the contemporary mystical writer, Annie Dillard, helps us to notice the mystery of nature's detailed complexity and intricacy.[7] Her approach to nature has been described as praying with her eyes open. She looked up and about, began to see, and was filled with wonder before creation. We then notice for the first time when we do that, Annie says, the way a wave rises above the ocean horizon, translucent and shot with lights. We listen to the mockingbird and not only puzzle at its song, but ponder the question, "Why is it beautiful?" As we pray in this way, the realization deepens that creation is God's possession rather than ours. Because it is God's, no one should be deprived of its fruits; nor should we hoard its gifts. Justice belongs to the poor and oppressed because the earth and all that belongs to it is God's. Our tendency to sever God from creation, relegating our prayer to a private compartment of life, allows the ecological, technological and nuclear threats to our world to go unchecked.

In her book, *Models of God*, theologian Sallie McFague suggests another form of meditation that is in keeping with love of the earth, a way of prayer that brings to consciousness the wonder of being.[8] Most efforts to raise our awareness of the dangers of destroying the environment or of nuclear war ask us to think big, she says, that is, they paint a picture of a devastating nuclear winter or the massive death and destruction that will occur if we maintain our present course. Such scenarios do remind us that war is not only violence against people; war is also against the earth. However, McFague recommends that we also think small, that we call up concrete images of specific events, people, plants and animals, objects and places that are precious to us. Then we are to dwell upon the uniqueness and value of these particular cherished aspects of our world, to meditate on them until the pain of contemplating their loss, not just to you or me, but to all life for all time, becomes unbearable.

When leading a group in this form of meditation, I have sometimes asked them to mention out loud the object of their contemplation in the silence that follows the prayer. Cherished aspects of our existence range over many areas: the smile on the face of a three-year-old daughter, a blossoming plum tree in the backyard, the sound of human laughter, the whistling of the wind in tree tops, the gestures a friend makes when she is excited, the quiet surface of a favorite lake in the mountains, the aroma of home-made bread as it comes from the oven.

Such a way of meditating gives rise to psalms for our time. The Hebrew psalms frequently dwell in a similar way in praise and thanksgiving on the details of creation: dark, misty rain clouds; thornbushes and thistles; grass on the mountainside; snow, frost and hail.

> You crown the year with your bounty,
> abundance flows wherever you pass;
> the desert pastures overflow,
> the hillsides are wrapped in joy,
> the meadows are dressed in flocks,
> the valleys are clothed in wheat,
> what shouts of joy, what singing!
> (Ps 65:11-13)

Many of the Psalms convey this integrity of the earth, the fact that the whole creation is good and every part of it counts.

From a Change of Heart to Action

On December 22, 1988, Chico Mendes was assassinated by Brazilian landowners seeking to turn increasingly larger sections of the Brazilian rain forest into farmland. Mendes was a rubber tapper who had gained worldwide attention for his defense of his fellow rubber tappers and all the human, animal and plant life threatened by the destruction of the rain forests. He was the president of the National Union of Rubbertappers, with about 70,000 members across the Amazon region. Under Chico's leadership, the rubbertappers and their families defended the forests in non-violent actions. They confronted and blocked the bulldozers and chain-saws by making human chains around threatened trees in the forest. In 1988 the United Nations had given him a major environmental award. He was also a member of a basic Christian community who sought to live the Word of God and put it into action. The greed of a few big "developers" gunned him down. Mendes' martyrdom challenges all of us. He was willing to put his life on the line for what he believed.

Concern for both the ecology and the poor calls for a change of lifestyle by affluent countries who must do less consuming and more sharing. Our values must change, and this is a spiritual issue. It is clear that we will need to practice restraint if other species and other peoples are going to survive on this earth. To do so we must be deeply convinced that God's purpose in creating is that we *all* find here a home that we can enjoy.

Crucial to this approach to life is an appropriate asceticism. It enables us to distinguish between what we need and what is unnecessary and ex-cessive. We become less careless and wasteful in relation to creation, aware of those who do not have enough to fill their basic human needs. Our life-styles of disconnected consumption give way to styles marked by simplicity and concern for the planetary community. In our consuming we take care to notice the effects our purchases have on the total creation: whether we choose one product or another at the grocery store; how much waste we create and how we recycle or dispose of it; our use of water, and our responsibility for polluting the air. These are daily ways of acknow-ledging that the earth is God's gift to be preserved wth gratitude. As we learn to relate to the earth as steward, friend and tender of a fragile garden, our actions large and small will begin to reflect that transformed relation-ship.

Notes

1. Elizabeth Dobson Gray develops this point in *Green Paradise Lost* (Wellesley, MA: Roundtable Press, 1979).

2. See *For Creation's Sake. Preaching, Ecology, and Justice,* ed. Dieter T. Hessel (Philadelphia: The Geneva Press, 1985); *Tending the Garden: Essays on the Gospel and the Earth,* ed. Wesley Granberg-Michaelson (Grand Rapids, MI: Wm B. Eerdmans Publishing Co., 1987); and Wesley Granberg-Michaelson, *A Worldly Spirituality. The Call to Redeem Life on Earth* (San Francisco: Harper and Row Publishers, 1984).

3. (Lincoln: University of Nebraska Press, 1961), p. 43.

4. (Boston: Beacon Press, 1986), p. 1.

5. *The Sacred Hoop,* p. 56.

6. *Hymn of the Universe* (New York: Harper & Row, 1965), pp. 19-37.

7. This vision is conveyed, for example, in *Pilgrim At Tinker Creek* (New York: Harper & Row Publishers, 1974); and *Teaching A Stone to Talk* (New York: Harper & Row Publishers, 1982).

8. (Philadelphia: Fortress Press, 1987), p. 187.

5

One Human Family

The space shuttles which have been launched during our era provide
visual images for what we know but constantly forget. From the perspective of outer space it is unmistakable that we all live on one small fragile
planet. As a shuttle completes its orbit around the earth, it draws a circle.
It encircles the planet, and in doing so demonstrates visually that the earth
is a continuum. We are one people. From the perspective of the space
shuttle we can see clearly the connections that are often lost to us at close
range. Nations and continents appear as wholes. It is evident that we share
one sea and one sky with plants, animals and people on other stretches of
the globe. One ocean chain and one atmosphere unite us. These images
from space remind us that no spirituality is adequate for our time unless it
embraces the entire planet. No matter where we live on the earth, our
spirituality must be global in scope.

The fourteenth-century hermitess, Julian of Norwich, provides another
image for this sense of the whole. Julian's teachings center on an appreciation of the goodness of God's created world. She uses imagery that weaves
elements from nature—spring rain, seaweed swept by the movement of
waves—with reflections on the divine. In one of her most familiar passages, she says that God showed her a little object, the size of a hazelnut.
She held it in the palm of her hand, and it was round as a ball. She puzzled,
wondering what it might be. The answer came: "It is all that is made."

Living out of these images of planetary oneness nurtures several elements of a global spirituality: 1) awareness that we are world citizens; 2)

51

concern for the liberation of all peoples; and 3) a willingness to act with global awareness at the local level. Let us look at each of these in turn.

Citizens of the World

In his speech to the Athenian Council of Areopagus, as described in Acts 17:26 and 28, Paul speaks of God as the one who has given life and breath to everyone. Further, Paul says, this God is not far from any one of us for it is in God that we live and move and have our being; God is the being who is most fully in relation. Paul pictures the entire human race—persons of all colors, religions, and political and economic systems—as living, moving, and existing in the cosmic womb of God. In this womb of God we know darkness and obscurity as well as warmth and nourishment.

Advances in travel and technology have increased our awareness of the reality Paul describes. Technology, for example, makes the world a single system in which what takes place in one part of the planet has an impact—sometimes a direct and immediate impact—on other places. Satellite communications make possible the instantaneous transmission of images and ideas throughout the world. Yet the development of technology and the mobility of populations can disrupt human bonds, causing us to feel disconnected from one another. Intercontinental ballistic missiles threaten the destruction of virtually any part of the globe from any other part. Our connections do not yet constitute a global community. Science has made notable achievements, but it has not been able to unify the world. That remains a goal. It will require the best resources of our minds and imaginations. It will also require the spiritual vision Paul provides when he speaks of our existence in the one womb of God.

Some years ago Teilhard de Chardin warned us that the age of nations was past, that the task before us now, if we wished to survive, was to build our common earth. He was challenging us to make a leap of imagination from local loyalties which isolate nation from nation to a vision of a diverse and interdependent world. Nationalism can inspire a fierce loyalty even to a nation which we may both love and hate, fostering competitive selfishness in relation to other nations. The lack of communication which results from different perspectives leads to estrangement and hostility. We habitually focus on narrow national interests, unconcerned about the immense misery and suffering in many parts of the world. Occasionally, when famine devastates Africa or flooding occurs in Bangladesh, a vision of a wider world breaks into our awareness. As one woman in the Soviet Union said during the devastating 1988 earthquake in Armenia: "When a tragedy like this hits, we set aside our petty quarrels and realize that we are all one human community." The challenge is to sustain that conviction at other times.

The survival of our planet will be achieved only at a price, and that price may be the abandonment of traditional kinds of patriotism. This need not mean relinquishing the roots that give us identity and cultural richness. We will still retain our uniqueness; we are American or Russian, French or German, Chinese or Japanese. What changes is our attitude toward diversity. Rather than being a cause for division and oppression, diversity is seen as a contribution to the richness of the whole. We realize that others in the world are like us but not identical to us. We no longer see them as objects of aggression, but as potential partners in cooperation. The sacrifices formerly made for our nation are now directed to the good of the world. We let go of false security and isolationism, the illusion that geographical boundaries can provide economic well-being and invulnerability. We place the good of humanity above our own national interests, learning to transcend narrow loyalties to color, class, religion, and culture when the common good requires it.

The Liberation of All Peoples

A spirituality rooted in our interdependence with peoples throughout the globe is already emerging. It is being born not so much in the writings of theologians as in the slums and shantytowns of non-Western parts of the world. It is coming from the experience of those considered "nonpersons." It is evolving, for example, from the experience of millions of people in Central America who are trying to make sense, from the viewpoint of the

Bible, of the oppressive circumstances in which they find themselves. This spirituality is based on the conviction that the whole planet earth, in its entirety, is the context of our spirituality. We cannot be unconcerned about the immense human misery and suffering in many parts of the world—situations, for example, where malnutrition is standard; where infant mortality is high; where people live in filthy conditions with no clean water, no jobs for adults and no schools for their children. This spirituality not only recognizes the connections, but exposes the darker side of these connections. It calls us to acknowledge that this world system is one of unjust relationships in which a small number benefit at the expense of the rest. Global holiness calls for meditation on our world, on the agony of human beings within it, and God's desire for the liberation of all.

An understanding of the Christian community as Christ's body deepens our awareness of these global connections. When one member suffers, all parts feel the suffering. When a member rejoices, it is cause for rejoicing in the total body. Members of Christ's body exist in all parts of the globe; we are a world church.[1] This provides a network of knowledge and action that would not otherwise be easily available to us. Our spirituality can be enriched by any of the local churches of the world. The church in the West is called on to support the movements toward liberation of churches in the Third World. In turn it is challenged to a fresh reading of the gospel, to conversion on many levels, and to a clearer understanding of what it is to be church. As in other areas of life, the shifts required by this new perspective can be threatening as well as enriching. Accustomed to a position of leadership and primary influence, the church in the West is disinclined to acknowledge the aspirations and insights of other local churches. It requires a profound letting go on many levels.

Seeing ourselves as world citizens means working to redeem a world system concerned primarily with borders and boundaries. Refugee camps are one indication of the injustice of this system. They represent our attempt to distance and define people as strangers, as the other. We have worked with these displaced persons ourselves, or seen them on our T.V. screens and in our newspapers. They are the people of Central America who are fleeing war and torture; the citizens of Jamaica displaced by a killer hurricane; the poor of Mexico left homeless by floods and earthquakes; the boat people of Vietnam, displaced by war and economic upheaval; those in our own country left homeless by poverty or illness. The world refugee problem deeply affects Asia, Africa and Latin America. Tens of millions of displaced persons are on the move in our world. The refugee has become a potent symbol of our time, indicative of the countless people who can find no secure home on our planet.

A constant biblical theme points to God as the owner of creation and its resources. This is especially true of the land.[2] Land is the principal wealth-producing resource in biblical times. Every fifty years it is to be redistributed in order to correct inequalities that develop over time (Lev 25:10). The theological principle that undergirds this year of jubilee is that God owns the land. The land is intended to be a blessing for all its inhabitants; those who work it are stewards and caretakers of a gift. They are sojourners with God.

> The land shall not be sold in perpetuity; for
> the land is mine, and you are but aliens who
> have become my tenants. Therefore, in every
> part of the country that you occupy, you must
> permit the land to be redeemed (Lev 25:23-24).

Amos and Isaiah condemn the concentration of landholdings that results in economic injustice and spiritual brokenness (Am 5; Is 3:12-15; 5:8-10). The Bible never sanctions the idea that the land is our own private possession to be used as we please. Rather, the land is a gift, a loan, given not to us as individuals but to all people. What would happen to the global economy if this idea were ever taken seriously?

Action at the Local Level

Diversity often leads to stereotypes, abstract generalizations that we attribute to those different from us. The Russians are out to destroy us, we say; Orientals are inscrutable. Gay persons want to abuse our children and destroy our families. Direct knowledge of others can shatter these stereotypes, revealing the commonalities that transcend differences. Even a brief glimpse of these connections can begin the process of change in us. My husband and I experienced such a moment while traveling through Malaysia. On a one-day train trip from Butterworth to Singapore, we were the only non-Asians in a car filled with Chinese, Indian, and Malaysian families. Two Chinese teenagers were in the seat directly in front of us. Late in the afternoon they began eating some fruit they had brought along as a snack. I marveled at the shape and color of it and tapped one of the girls on the shoulder, gesturing to indicate that I wanted to know the fruit's name. Both girls immediately wanted to share it with me. When I demurred at their offer, one of them said, "Treat, treat," and held out pieces of the fruit for me and my husband. We thanked them as they showed us how to break open the skin to reach the sweet center within. Meanwhile others on the train had observed us and came forward to offer us various tropical fruits, including two of the smallest bananas I had ever seen. We spoke little of one another's languages, but we shared a moment of fun and friendship in spite of that. It was a brief experience and did not remove the difficulty of international relations, but I carry it with me as a metaphor of what might be possible on a larger scale.

Recently another couple and their two young daughters spent eleven months traveling around the globe, spending most of their time in the Third World. Their goal was to get rid of prejudices and preconceptions through personal exposure to the diversity of peoples and cultures in the world. They traveled independently, using public transportation and staying mostly in guest houses and private homes. The people in each of the places they visited became their teachers, opening their eyes to new ways of looking at the world. They became aware of the harsh realities that most people face—poverty, exploitation, displacement, and environmental destruction. The world became a school for them. But more than that. It is now their home; they have loved many places and peoples around the globe and been loved in return.

It is not possible or necessary for most of us to travel around the globe in order to realize that we are one human family. We are surrounded every day by challenges presented by cultural, religious, and economic diversity.

Many opportunities for increased understanding remain untapped by us because we fear what is different. A spiritual quality intrinsic to nonviolent unification is openness to dialogue. A dialogue is a conversation in which we hold out the hope of reaching the other individual or group, of breaking through barriers in order to come to new understanding or the resolution of a problem. It is a spiritual discipline required for planetary survival.

For all of us at times, awareness of the scale of suffering in the world is a cause for despair, not an incentive to action. We cannot bear the endless saga of human pain. Pondering problems on a global scale makes them appear simply overwhelming; one wonders where to begin. The complex problems of war and world hunger, the scale of the suffering attendant on natural disasters such as earthquakes and flooding, leave us feeling powerless and hopeless. Further the massive technology that connects us with others in the world also blurs the exact nature of those connections. When we purchase bananas at the grocery store, for example, many of us know little or nothing about the international cartels that set the price for bananas. We have little awareness of the political repression and land-ownership patterns the system imposes, or the illnesses suffered by the banana workers and their families due to the imposed use of pesticides.

Awareness of global connections need not simply extend the scope of problems so that they become overwhelming. It can also underscore the importance of each individual action we undertake. Interdependence creates a sense of responsibility, but it is also a foundation of hope and courage. It reminds us that we do not carry the whole weight; we are with others in this effort. The metaphor of a stone thrown into a pond, producing ever-widening circles, is often used to illustrate these relationships.

When faced with the immensity of world problems, it helps me to remember that each of us exists within a certain ring of primary influences—our families, friends, and neighbors—but that each of those primary influences in turn has its own ring of influences. These partially overlap and partially extend beyond the circles of the others. Influences beyond my immediate sphere are mediated to me through those that are close. For example, I do not work directly with the people of Peru. However, I have a close friend who does. Through this friend I have come to know and care about the Peruvian people: their loss of family members to terrorist attacks, their projects to dig wells, their weekly meetings to share the gospels, their fiestas and celebrations. The circles widen. Some influences are direct, but many are indirect. Everything gradually affects everything else.

A group recently honored by the Seattle World Affairs Council exemplifies this approach. Calling themselves Ploughshares, this citizen group aims to foster better people-to-people communications internationally, especially with the Soviet Union. It was founded by a group of Peace Corps volunteers who wanted to work for more peace in the world in the same spirit they had known in their assignments years before. One of their successes was the building of a peace park in Tashkent, Seattle's sister city in the Soviet Union. Scores of Ploughshares volunteers worked there with Soviet volunteers. Hundreds of boosters in the United States helped to finance it. A new project will involve teams of Americans and Russians working together to erect shelters for needy people in the United States and then doing the same in the Soviet Union and in Third World nations.

What we become matters not only to ourselves; we make a difference in the entire universe. As an oppressed black Christian in South Africa commented, solidarity with the rest of the world church is very important. When you are sitting in a prison cell or being convinced by interrogators that you have been forgotten, knowing that there are Christians at home and abroad doing what they can to support you enables you to go on. This influence is strongest in our immediate circle, but somehow affects the rest of the universe. The more informed and intentional my intervention is, the more likely it is to have the effect I hope for. That is why research and analysis are such an important part of peace and justice work. They alert us to the realities which govern the world food market, for example, and indicate the kind of action that will make a difference.

The complexity of issues such as world hunger can serve as an excuse for inaction. But it should not. Many of the causes of hunger are easily identifiable and there are numerous avenues presented to us for action. While retaining a global vision, we need the conviction that we can act effectively at the local level, in the actual places where we live and work. A familiar adage summarizes this approach: Think globally; act locally. In addition, we need help in analyzing the impact our actions have on others. There are now many national and international organizations willing to supply us with both an analysis of the causes, and suggestions for simple actions. Pax Christi, Amnesty International, and Bread For the World are just a few of these.[3]

In his book *Planetary Theology*, the noted Asian theologian Tissa Balasuriya indicates a number of long-term goals for those of us concerned with a global spirituality.[4] We have already referred to some of these goals: an end to the arms race and the despoiling of nations, the adoption of a simpler life-style by the affluent, and the redistribution of resources and land among people. Balasuriya believes we also need to work toward a world authority and the subordination of the use of technology to human needs and rights. All these goals suggest actions we could begin even now on a local level. The household of the faith has become the planetary household, and our spirituality calls us to recognize our responsibility for putting this house in order.

Notes

1.   See Walter Bühlmann, *The Coming of the Third Church* (Maryknoll, NY: Orbis Books, 1977).

2.   Walter Brueggemann develops this theme in *The Land* (Philadelphia: Fortress Press, 1977); and John Hart treats it in *The Spirit of the Earth—A Theology of the Land* (New York: Paulist Press, 1984).

3.   Resources and suggestions for becoming involved in action groups can be found in Adam Daniel Corson-Finnerty, *World Citizen: Action for Global Justice* (Maryknoll, NY: Orbis Books, 1982). See also Jack Nelson-Pallmeyer, *The Politics of Compassion* (Maryknoll, NY: Orbis Books, 1986).

4.   (Maryknoll, NY: Orbis Books, 1984).

6

The Compassion of God

A quiet but significant shift is taking place in the way we understand
God's relationship to our world. Traditional explanations have stressed that
though we are changed by our relationship with the divine, God is not really affected by our joys and sufferings. During recent decades theologians
have begun to speak of a suffering, compassionate God. Dietrich Bonhoeffer, the young Lutheran pastor executed in 1945 in an extermination camp
at Flossenburg, introduces the theme in a letter from his prison cell in July
of 1944.[1] He speaks of the powerlessness and suffering of God, declaring
that only a suffering God can help. This God, Bonhoeffer believes, is the
God of the Bible.

Bonhoeffer's suggestion has been expanded by others who question
whether the affirmation of God's perfection actually demands a God who
is absolutely self-sufficient and self-contained, a God not really affected by
what happens in our world.[2] This would never be our ideal of perfection in
another human being. Why should it be so for God? What if divine compassion were seen not as a defect in God's perfection but as the highest expression of God's perfection? In a world where relationship and connection characterize all of reality, a God who is more fully related to all of
creation than any other being is perfect in a way that commands our ad-
miration and inspires our imitation. Perfection becomes a way of speaking
about the divine sensitivity and relatedness. Theologian Daniel Day Wil-
liams situates this belief within the meaning of divine immanence and
transcendence: God is vulnerable to the world's misery yet invulnerable to
ultimate defeat.[3]

To speak of the suffering of God is to affirm that God is love. The personal metaphors we use for God—father, mother, lover, friend—all describe a love that cares. When we call God friend, for example, we express our confidence that God is a companion who accompanies us in both joy and suffering. A friend is one who enters into our feelings, hurts when we are in pain, and rejoices in our happiness. As a way of imaging this, the philosopher Alfred North Whitehead speaks of God as "the great companion—the fellow-sufferer who understands."[4] To speak of God as friend is to affirm that we are not alone as we struggle against the forces of sin and evil.

The experience of God's love is the foundation of Christian spirituality. It is therefore important to understand in what sense it is possible to speak of the divine suffering and compassion. We will look first at its biblical meaning and then its significance for our prayer and action.

The Biblical Witness to God's Compassion

When we experience loss and disappointment, the first questions that come to us are, Why is this happening to me? Why should I have to suffer? The Bible does not speculate much about the origin of evil. Rather, it stresses God's response to suffering and calls us to work against it ourselves. The most profound dimension of that divine response is compassion.

The Exodus event is often regarded as a paradigm for God's character and activity in history. God is portrayed in Exodus not only as noticing the suffering of the Hebrew slaves in Egypt, but as identifying with their agony. God knows the Hebrews' situation and responds by leading them to liberation.

> I have witnessed the affliction of my people in Egypt and have heard their cry of complaint against their slave drivers, so I know well what they are suffering (Ex 3:7).

God's love is responsive.

Other biblical texts also describe a God of compassion. Isaiah depicts God as a woman in the process of giving birth.

> God speaks: "From the beginning I have been silent, I have kept quiet, held myself in check. I groan like a woman in labor, I suffocate, I stifle" (42:14).

Isaiah's image reveals a God present with those who are oppressed by the pain of our world. This agony and tragedy are taken into the divine life where they are healed and transformed. A new world is born from God's travail, a world in which the blind, the lame and the imprisoned are set free.

The prophet Jeremiah speaks in similar images during the time of Israel's exile. In a passage which evokes Israel's pain during that period, God consoles Rachel as she mourns the loss of Ephraim.

> Is Ephraim my dear Son? my darling child?
> For the more I speak of him,
> the more do I remember him.
> Therefore, my womb trembles for him;
> I will truly show motherly compassion
> upon him (Jer 31:20).

In his book, *The Prophets*, the late Jewish rabbi Abraham Heschel wrote at length of the pathos of God as portrayed in prophets like Isaiah and Jeremiah.[5] This divine pathos, Heschel believed, is grounded in an intimate, personal relationship with the covenant community. It points to the dynamic character of God's interaction with the community. At the same time, awareness of God's transcendence reminds us of the limits of any language used for the divine.

> For my thoughts are not your thoughts,
> my ways not your ways—it is God who speaks.
> Yes, the heavens are as high above the earth
> as my ways are above your ways,
> my thoughts above your thoughts (Is 55:8-9).

In other words, we are warned that all human words about God are only partial and tentative attempts to flesh out the divine mystery.

Suffering in human experience can threaten our integrity and deaden our sensitivity. We feel at times that we have moved beyond the limits of our strength. Suffering in God cannot be seen in just the same way, since we are speaking in analogy whenever we use human experience to describe God. Suffering is not a pain or deprivation which threatens God's integrity or purpose. It is God's acceptance of the tragic element in creation, a bearing with creation's loss and failure and a being moved to the need for redemptive action. God knows all possible outcomes, the limits of all tragedy, and the infinite resources for dealing with every evil. Suffering is therefore transformed in God. God shares in the world's suffering, but without all the limitations that mark finite sufferers. God's creative vision is not changed, but God is moved by our pain and works in and through us as we suffer.

The prophetic hope for our world finds its fulfillment in Jesus. The incarnation has always been clear evidence of God's love and concern for humanity. John's epistles declare simply that "God is love." Jesus' ministry was characterized by identification with the poor and oppressed, the outcast and alienated of society.

> Jesus lamented, "Jerusalem, Jerusalem, you that kill the prophets and stone those who are sent to you! How often have I longed to gather your children, as a hen gathers her chicks under her wings, and you refused" (Lk 13:34).

Since Jesus reveals who God is for us, it is hard to think of this God as someone unmoved and unaffected by the sufferings of the world. Jesus' death on the cross witnesses to the extent of God's compassion, to the fact that God suffers with us in our sufferings.

If the passion and compassion of God are stressed in the biblical accounts, how did the Christian tradition come to focus exclusively on the unchangeableness of God? The answer lies in the influence of Greek metaphysics. In the Greek world view, perfection is equated with the unchanging; to be moved by another's pain would signify a limitation. Under Greek influence the passionate, dynamic God of the Bible is transformed gradually into Aristotle's unmoved mover. Relying on this tradition Thomas Aquinas wrote, for example, that God loves without passion. God's love is shown by doing good things for us; our love is responsive, but the divine love is purely creative. In other words, it is a love that affects others but is not affected in turn.

How would turning from this Greek notion of perfection and returning to the biblical God of compassion influence our prayer and action?

The Compassion of God and Christian Spirituality

Suffering of any kind poses a critical challenge to our spiritual lives. I see this especially in my work with the frail elderly. A woman who has been a faithful friend of God for eight or nine decades of life now faces a level of diminishment that seems senseless and useless. She has lost her husband and her home of many years. Her eyesight is failing and she knows the nagging pain of chronic arthritis. She prays. Nothing seems to happen. Where is God, she wonders? At such times older people often remark to me: "I don't think God cares," or "I think God has forgotten me." Their relationship with God is at risk.

We recognize the experience of this older woman as our own. Suffering and tragedy threaten to erode our relationship with God, too; they give rise to gnawing doubts about God's care for us, God's fairness in the face of the unequal distribution of suffering, God's ability or willingness to come to our aid.

Self-help books tell us how to grieve our losses, how to begin again after a disaster, how to find strength in other people and activities. What a spirituality addresses that many of these books do not, is the relationship of God to our loss. For the believer, that question is foundational and underlies all the other concerns. Does God want me to resign myself to this pain

The Compassion of God 65

as coming from the divine will? Can I turn to God for comfort if God is the one who sent this tragedy into my life in the first place? Is there reason to hope that God can remove this pain from my life, and should I pray for that? Does God care about my sufferings? Might it even be true to say that God suffers with me, in the words of a woman from Central America, that God weeps with me in my pain?

In my experience of being with others who are suffering or dying, I have found that there are many things that cannot be changed. Often neither they nor I can alter the situation. We cannot bring back the husband killed in a car accident. We cannot restore the house destroyed by fire. We cannot, in many cases, cure the cancer or stop the progress of multiple sclerosis. We cannot turn back the ravaging flood or hurricane. Nor do rational explanations offer much comfort when we are in the midst of a loss. In easier times, we might reason that a God who allows no pain and no grief also allows no choice. We might understand that suffering and evil are not caused by God but result from creation and humanity's freedom, that this freedom means there is randomness in life, that some freedom must exist if creation is to be genuinely distinct from God. But rational explanations are small comfort in the midst of a loss. What we need is a presence that lifts the suffering into the context of relationship, that brings the pain into the circle of community where we can be supported, comforted, and enlivened by hope. The ground of this circle of caring and hope is a compassionate God.

I need to know that God stands with me against this evil and suffering, that I am not alone as I struggle with it. God does not send it to test or educate me, rather God is "the fellow-sufferer who understands."

> Even though I walk in the dark valley
> I fear no evil; for you are at my side
> With your rod and your staff
>   that give me courage (Ps 23:4).

It is this deep intuition that God is with us in our pain that accounts, I think, for the widespread love of Psalm 23 as a prayer in times of trouble.

The relationship of suffering to God concerns not only the compassion, but also the passion, of God. Can God feel our pain, anguish, sorrow and disappointment about the human situation? We have removed all feeling from God only because someone's ideal of perfection was of a rational being. In the past it was believed that feelings interfere with clear, rational thought and are therefore of a lesser order than thinking. But this creates a number of problems in the spiritual life. First, when the model of our love is a divine love that is passionless and devoid of feeling, we find it hard to find a place in spirituality for strong emotions. Passionate love, rather than being one of the avenues to God, is looked upon as a distraction and danger. When these attitudes prevail, it is hard to be ourselves before God. We hold back the deepest and most complex of our emotions because they seem somehow unworthy of God—the desire we feel for another; the anger, even rage, we find in ourselves; the near-despair that arises as we struggle with life. But if God is a God of passion and compassion, a God who feels our emotions and who is more sensitive than anyone else with whom we relate, then our prayer can be fully honest. Such honesty is characteristic of many forms of biblical prayer, but above all of that form known as lament.

Biblical laments are a voice for our time, a prayer for believers in situations of sorrow where there can be no pretense or whitewashing of feelings. Laments reflect a relationship with God which searches for reasons and understanding, which is often pain-filled, and which nonetheless awaits change with a spirit that is daring and hopeful. What is more, lament gives tangibility to the unformulated anguish we feel, bringing it to expression so that it can be worked through.

> Worn out from weeping are my eyes,
>   within me all is in ferment;
> My gall is poured out on the ground
>   because of the downfall of the
>   daughter of my people.
> As child and infant faint away
>   in the open spaces of the town (Lm 2:11).

God, my God, I call for help all day,
I weep to you all night;
  may my prayer reach you;
  hear my cries for help;

for my soul is troubled,
my life is on the brink of Sheol;
I am numbered among those who go down to the Pit,
a person bereft of strength. . . .

God, I invoke you all day,
I stretch out my hands to you:
are your marvels meant for the dead,
can ghosts rise up to praise you?
                    (Ps 88:1-4; 9-10).

These laments reflect a profound, searching, troubled relationship with God, one based on the freedom to express honest emotions.

Yet compassion is more than a feeling. If it leads to no action, it is empty. God seeks to liberate us. And God calls us to join in the divine struggle against suffering. Paul says that because we have encountered the God of compassion and comfort we are able to comfort others in turn (2 Cor 1:4). If God stands against evil, we cannot simply resign ourselves to it as God's will. We must struggle with God against it. God is redemptively at work in the world to heal wounds and enable the emergence of the new. Only when we have done all we can to eliminate suffering, can we transform its meaning into a redemptive one. The novelist Flannery O'Connor drew strength from this insight in dealing with the disease of lupus that finally claimed her life. She learned the truth from the writings of Teilhard de Chardin. She liked what Teilhard wrote, she said, about doing all that you could to rid yourself and the world of suffering before you attempted to reach resignation.[6]

Belief in the compassion of God affects our spiritual life in another way. Compassion is the ability to hear and understand another's experience and respond to it. It is the flow of energy that moves between us and others in the world, the shared experience that allows our lives to affect and be affected by others. Compassion presupposes mutuality; such mutuality is the goal of God's commitment to human persons—that we will come to love as we have been loved.

It has been commonplace in Western spirituality to depict the highest form of love as utterly heedless of self. We imagine the saint to be completely devoid of self-concern. Women, especially, have been encouraged to reach complete self-denial in their love for others. This idealization of selfless love rests on a misunderstanding of divine love, which is offered as the perfect example toward which human love should strive. It also rests on an interpretation of self-abnegation as the key to Jesus' life. The fourteenth-century Dutch monastic Thomas à Kempis extolled the love expressed by Jesus as free of all self-interest and self-love. He believed this was the Christian ideal.

But this is too simple a depiction of the complex emotions that marked Jesus' love. Jesus clearly wanted his love to be accepted and reciprocated. He lamented that people "did not recognize God's moment when it came" (Lk 19:44). The gospels reflect his concern for both himself and his Father: "I came accredited by my Father, and you have no welcome for me" (Jn 5:43). Like the God of Israel, Jesus longed for the return of his love. Jesus showed us exemplary patience and forgiveness, but these are not the same as selflessness. They do not negate mutuality as the highest goal of love; rather, they are necessary precisely because this goal has been violated. The tragedy is that Jesus' love is not returned. Human freedom thwarts the mutuality Jesus desires and strives to bring about.

But if God not only affects but is affected by others, if God responds as well as initiates, we have a different way of imaging the highest ideal of love. Mutuality, not mere giving, now becomes the ideal. Complete self-abnegation leaves a person unattached in any essential way to the community. The love we most deeply want and need is mutual love, a kind of love that has the quality of love given and love received. It is in mutual love that we experience joy, a sense of well-being and identity, and an affirmation of the self which encourages the giving of the self. This is an interpersonal understanding of love in which both the "I" and the "Thou" are the recipients of love as well as its sources. It is through this kind of love, not complete selflessness or utter disregard of self, that we live out the image of God.[7]

The ideal of love stands at the heart of the gospel and of Christian spirituality. As we reclaim the biblical understanding of the compassion and passion of God, it will transform the way we see both suffering and love in our spiritual lives. Each will find their deepest meaning in a community of mutual care and healing, rooted in God's presence at the center of those relationships. As the Exodus story tells us, God is not above us but with us on the journey as we join together, as we suffer and endure in the desert, and as we rejoice in and celebrate our sources of sustenance and faith on our way to the Promised Land.

Notes

1.   (New York: The Macmillan Co., 1972), pp. 360-361.

2.   See Warren McWilliams, *The Passion of God. Divine Suffering in Contemporary Protestant Theology* (Macon, GA: Mercer University Press, 1985); and Paul S. Fiddes, *The Creative Suffering of God* (London: Oxford University Press, 1988).

3.   *The Spirit and the Forms of Love* (New York: Harper & Row Publishers, 1968).

4.   *Process and Reality*, p. 413.

5.   (New York: Harper & Row Publishers, 1962).

6.   *The Habit of Being*, ed. Sally Fitzgerald (New York: Random House, 1979), p. 509.

7.   See Beverly Harrison, "Human Sexuality and Mutuality," *Christian Feminism. Visions of a New Humanity*, ed. Judith L. Weidman (San Francisco: Harper & Row Publishers, 1984), pp. 141-157.

7

An Embodied Spirituality

Of all the broken connections which need healing, that between body and spirit is among the most fundamental to Christian spirituality. Past spiritual systems have severed spirit from body, rejecting the latter, leaving us hungry for a wholeness many of us have never known. We are now recovering the truth that the material and the spiritual are not separate compartments of existence, but two different facets of the same reality.

Sometimes we catch a glimpse of this integrity, of the mysterious unity of body and spirit that characterizes human existence. It often comes to me while watching small children playing at the ocean. Standing at a distance I cannot hear their voices. But their bodies convey all the delight and excitement they experience as they watch the waves and build structures in the sand. As the water rolls toward them, they leap and turn, scurrying back toward safety. Encounters with a dog along the beach or efforts to make a kite fly produce stamps of impatience or heads thrown back in laughter and freedom. They witness to the truth that human beings are incarnate spirit.

Contemporary spirituality is trying to recover this experience of wholeness, along with the sense of joy and well-being it produces. We now understand better how the tradition developed which separated body and spirit. We are also rediscovering ways of thinking and living that can help heal the divorce. These include 1) a new way of envisioning the body in relation to the self; 2) a fresh understanding of the relationship between sexuality and spirituality; and 3) more creative approaches to Christian asceticism.

Body and Self

How am I related to my body? To answer this question, we will first look briefly at the way it is approached in Greek thinking. Then we will draw insights from Paul's writings in the New Testament, from the meaning of the incarnation itself, and from the insights of some contemporary philosophers.

The Greek philosophers Socrates and Plato established for much of Western spirituality the primacy of the soul. The soul, they believed, was only incidentally associated with the body. Those aspects of life connected with the soul, such as mind and intellect, were considered separate from and superior to those related to the body, such as biological needs and emotions. The physical, in its various forms—nature, the human body, sexuality—was considered somehow evil, polluted, and inimical to religious experience. The body and nature were to be conquered and controlled.

In contrast to this Greek approach, Paul in his epistles describes a dialectic, not between soul and body, but between spirit and flesh—and Paul's terms do not mean soul and body at all. The terms spirit and flesh describe two different *directions* for our lives. Spirit connects us to the source of life and being; flesh leads us to immediate pleasure and enjoyment. When speaking of both flesh and spirit Paul is describing ways in which we relate to our bodies. The way of the flesh seeks goals that cannot really provide happiness; spirit seeks a different set of goals, and finds integrity and happiness.

> It is obvious what proceeds from the flesh: fornication, gross indecency and sexual irresponsibility; idolatry and sorcery; feuds and wrangling, jealousy, bad temper and quarrels; disagreements, factions, envy, drunkenness, orgies and similar things. I warn you now, as I warned you before: those who behave like this will not inherit the reign of God.

> In contrast, the fruit of the spirit is love, joy, peace, patience, kindness, goodness, trustfulness, gentleness and self-control (Gal 5:19-23).

Following the flesh creates dismemberment and pain; it distorts our fundamental unity. The life of the Spirit allows us to walk again in this oneness.

For Paul, "flesh" is not the body at all. The body means what is essentially whole or can become so; the body is the dwelling place of the Spirit. Paul uses the term body collectively as well as individually, moving freely from one meaning to another. At one time he speaks of the "individual" body; at another, of the redemption of "our" body. In this way, body comes to connote all that human persons have in common, in spite of their individual differences. This body is what connects us to one another and the universe. "Flesh" creates human isolation and otherness by feuds, factions, envy, and sexual irresponsibility; body joins human beings together and is the subject of the resurrection.

We find a similar affirmation of the body when we turn to the Christian message of the incarnation. The incarnation tells us that God loves the human; God has entered into our life, a life that is bodily, sexual, and emotional. Through this we learn to appreciate that grace comes in bodily form. This truth contrasts with some of the messages we have absorbed about the sinfulness and inferiority of the body. Because of these messages, many of us are ashamed of our bodies and sometimes even hate them. But it is only through the body that we can feel and that we can express our selves and our relationships with others, even many aspects of our relationship with God. Incarnation is the mystery of divine embodiment. God comes to us in and through our material existence; so, too, we must relate to God and to others in and through our bodiliness. Not only our belief in the incarnation, but our conviction regarding a bodily resurrection and Christ's presence in the bread and wine of the eucharist, provides us with a bodily tradition of spirituality.

In contrast to Greek philosophy, which saw the soul as superior to the body, many contemporary philosophers depict the relationship between body and spirit as a dynamic one. Both are aspects of the same reality, not separate and distinct realities. Spirit and body exist on a continuum, for matter is not inanimate substance. Matter, as seen through the eyes of modern science, throbs with energy, and is in essential continuity with spirit.

The interaction between body and spirit takes on many dimensions and changes over a lifetime. People who are old and frail experience one aspect of this. At times they feel their spirits to be stronger and more vital than at any time in their lives; they have intense creativity. However, their bodies are declining and cannot supply the physical strength their plans would require. When we are ill or injured, we experience this same bodily pain and limitation. At other points in our lives the body seems stronger than the spirit. We lose our mental powers in diseases like Alzheimer's while we are still physically robust and strong. Such experiences deepen our sense of the mysterious connection between body and spirit.

The insights of Paul, the meaning of the incarnation, and contemporary philosophy's emphasis on the interrelatedness of body and spirit all bring us to a new way of answering the question, How am I related to my body? We exist as body/spirit unities; the human person is organically related to the body and at the same time transcends it. Since spirit and body exist on a continuum, we cannot say where one begins and the other ends. This way of viewing the body/spirit relationship illumines many aspects of our experience.

Our minds, even when dominant, are closely connected to bodily processes that either enhance our attention or frustrate and attenuate it. We all know what it is like to try to concentrate in a classroom when we are hungry, have a headache, or have been sitting too long. Concepts and theories alone do not enlighten or liberate, redeem or destroy. At the most profound level, our spirits are created and recreated in terms of physical energies of nature, which are most intimately experienced by the body.

We experience in many ways the fact that thoughts have bodily repercussions. I can make myself sick by the way I think. To recognize how true this is, we have only to recall the way our bodies respond when we tell ourselves before an exam, a performance, or a social event that we are not really good enough to face it, and will probably fail. Muscles tighten, energy drains away. Many current approaches to physical healing emphasize that mind and spirit must be enlisted to help heal the body. Learning to love, dealing with our anger so that it does not turn into hatred and resentment, finding a purpose for our lives—these all liberate powerful healing energy and restore bodily well-being.

This sense of permeable boundaries between body and spirit characterizes our relationship with all of creation. We cannot define where a body begins and where external nature ends. Consider for a moment an experience many of us have had. At one time or another we have felt ourselves merging with our surroundings. It may have happened during a walk in the woods or while contemplating a lake or waterfall. Perhaps it happened while standing before a great painting or sculpture. At such times we feel more fluid, less bounded than before. We are no longer so aware of our body as separating us as of uniting us with all else.

The realization that we are embodied prepares the way for a new appreciation of the place of emotions in the spiritual life. All our relationships—whether to God, others, or the cosmos—are mediated through our bodies. Our senses and feelings bring the world to us; our minds are affected by the way we relate physically to the world. Our understanding of God, for example, does not come primarily from doctrines and ideas. It is woven from our experience—our loves, hates, and fears. Our thoughts arise from the intense and complex feelings we know in our depths. When we feel bitterness or resentment, or when we are filled with joy and excitement, our task is not to push these feelings aside but to try to understand them, to listen to what they can teach us about our relationship with God and others.

Once we become convinced of the meaning of embodiment, we can no longer ask how questions of world hunger and justice relate to spirituality. Christians sometimes resent the introduction of these topics, believing them intrusions into the world of religion. But when we see body and spirit as different aspects of a unified reality, we understand the importance of bodily well-being to all in the world. In many parts of the earth the question of life itself, bodily life, is the major spiritual issue. If bodies are worth loving, then attention to the needs of bodily existence is a primary spiritual agenda. At the heart of an embodied spirituality is concern that all persons have the basic necessities of bodily existence, such as food and shelter.

An appreciation of the Christian meaning of embodiment also prepares us to understand the relationship between sexuality and spirituality. We turn now to that topic.

Sexuality and Spirituality

Some people are troubled by the very linking of sexuality with spirituality. This is not surprising since fear of sexuality is pervasive in the Christian tradition. This uneasiness stems from misunderstandings of both sexuality and spirituality.[1]

Sexuality is misunderstood when it is restricted to sex. Sexuality is thus reduced to the genital act; all other sensuous experiences are minimized. Actually, sexuality is much broader than this. As the power of personal attraction to others, it is integral to any spirituality. Sexuality is not one distinct aspect of life; it is, rather, the basis of our connection to all things, the foundation of our power to relate to others as female or male. It is not accidental that a society that misunderstands sexuality also has difficulty achieving communal wholeness.

We express our sexuality in all our friendships; in the way we parent, work, and play; in our relationship with God in prayer and worship. Sexuality is a way of describing at the human level what we have seen operating at all levels of life—an energy that produces a cosmic dance of mutual attraction. The more fully I integrate my sexuality into my personality, the more passion and energy there will be to give color and power to my life. Sexuality is that embodied energy which links us to others in communication and communion; it is our ability to affect and be affected by others. Sex is just one of many possible expressions of this energy.

Since it is the magnetism of relationship, sexuality becomes distorted
when it is unintegrated, disconnected from the truth and meaning of our
relationships. Disengaged sex, though often portrayed positively in the
media, is actually a contradiction in terms. Sex is truly joyful only when it
is incorporated into relationships and purposes that spring from my personal center, from who I really am in relationship to others.

Sex is, in fact, a most basic symbol for unity and our desire to be one.
Sex is a mode of knowledge, as the biblical writers make clear in referring
to intercourse as a way of knowing another. Too often we have focused on
the ways in which sex can go wrong, overlooking the very important fact
that sex is first of all a wonderful gift of God, a blessing meant to enhance
and deepen human life. We may have learned to equate sex with sin, but
there is nothing bad about sexual feelings and excitement. It is true that
sexual energy can hurt others, but all human energies can be used for evil
as well as good ends. In the biblical creation accounts, God is portrayed as
pronouncing sexual beings very good, part of the beauty and richness of
creation. As God's creation, sex is also an avenue to the sacred, one of the
ways in which we come to know the divine comfort and healing. When
we love and are loved well, we know what it is to be found valuable just as
we are, with all of our spots and wrinkles.

We need to name and understand our sexual hungers and passions, our
desires and longings. Unnamed, they remain outside our control; this
makes it difficult to integrate them into genuine caring for self and others.
These longings may be greater when we are lonely, and so remind us of
our deep need for love. Sex without love is empty, both for ourselves and
for others. Yet it is held up as exciting by a culture which often turns
people into sex objects. Sex then becomes a game of seduction, compul-
sion, or control. What we really want is sex that enhances our self-respect
and well-being and deepens our relations with others, sex that springs from
love, and leads both to deeper intimacy and to deeper self-regard.

A positive approach to the relationship between sexuality and
spirituality frees us to acknowledge the importance of sensuality and touch
in all of existence. Since we are embodied, we are sensual. Sensuality is
intrinsic to an incarnational spirituality. Because of our fear of sex and

sexuality, we mistrust the sensuous, regarding it as bordering on the bad. Being sensuous is, however, a way of deepening our connection with our bodies and the material creation. This leads, in turn, to praise and gratitude for the wonder of creation. The biblical Song of Songs is a sensuous book where we encounter the sights, smells, and textures of creation. The Song of Songs is sensuous not only because it celebrates human love, but because it rejoices in the bodily and the physical, blending sight, sound and sense. Its pages contain the aroma of spiced wine and myrrh and frankincense; the juice of pomegranates; the delights of human touch. In the first garden of creation, that of Eden, something went awry. We see humans there ill at ease with their bodies and one another, with nature and God. Here in the Song of Songs we have another garden, one filled with sensuous objects and praise of human bodiliness. In this redeemed garden persons are completely at home with pleasure and delight.

Human touch can be a sacrament of God's love and healing. Touch heals wounds and convinces us that we are lovable and beautiful. Touch can speak forgiveness more powerfully than words. At key points in our lives, bodily touch is the only way we can reach one another or convey the deepest dimensions of our relationships. A friend told me that her father and mother had developed a code of touch that became the only way they could communicate when her mother was dying of a stroke: two fingers tapped on the wrist three times meant I love you. Once I was privileged to be a part of a reconciliation that took place between two sisters who had not spoken to one another for over twenty years. A grievance between them had been allowed to harden and deepen until it created a chasm they thought it impossible to bridge. One of the sisters, Betty, was dying of cancer, and wanted to make peace before her death. She asked me to arrange for a visit with her sister. As the day approached for the visit, Betty talked to me about all the things she wanted to say to her sister—words of sorrow for her part in the misunderstanding, explanations of why she had waited so long to make contact. However, when the actual meeting took place, very few words were exchanged. Betty and her sister simply embraced one another and wept.

As we attempt to reintegrate the body into our spirituality, it is helpful to reflect on the way in which Jesus uses touch to heal. The gospels show us many examples of this: In healing the blind man, Jesus mixes dirt with his own spittle and presses it against the blind man's eyes (Jn 9:6-7). Jesus hugs children and gives them his blessing (Mk 10:16). He praises the woman who anoints him with a fragrant oil (Jn 12:1-8).

One story of such healing touch stands out as especially poignant. A hemorrhaging woman emerges from the great crowd that followed Jesus (Mk 5: 25-34). She is a bold woman, with strong faith. Mark recognizes the physical and social suffering this woman has endured for twelve years.

> After long and painful treatment under various doctors, she had spent all she had without being any the better for it; in fact, she was getting worse.

If I can touch even his clothes, the woman thinks, I will be well again. She touches his cloak. Jesus is aware that he has been touched in a special way; he feels his flow of power that stops her flow of blood, and confirms what she has experienced. Touch has healed her. We are incarnate spirit.

Helpful examples of the power of touch and sensuality are also found in Jacques Lusseyran's book, *And There Was Light.*[2] Lusseyran tells how he went blind at the age of eight and, as a result, came to see the world in a new way. He spent hours learning to really touch tomatoes, the walls of the house, the materials of curtains, or a clod of earth. Touching in this way became a way of tuning in to things, of allowing their current to connect with his own, as in electricity. Lusseyran says that in this way he stopped living in front of things and began living with them.

Christian Asceticism

A recurring theme in spiritual literature is that of self-denial or asceticism. Does asceticism still have a role in a spirituality that no longer views the body as evil? It does, but it is now based on recognition of our body/spirit unity and the interrelatedness of all life. The goal of asceticism today is not subjugation of our lesser bodily selves. Rather, asceticism is a means to personal wholeness and global solidarity. Underlying the notion of asceticism is the realization that limits are essential to personal and communal health and well-being. This is true on several different levels—that of daily decisions, of work for justice, and of artistic expression.

Asceticism demands a willingness to listen to our bodies. This attunement to the body may require a discipline of the mind. If we believe in the truth of incarnation and embodiment, we cannot ignore the messages about personal limits and well-being that our bodies give us. Refusal to listen when our bodies tell us that we are weary, in pain, or stressed beyond our limits destroys the physical resources that support our gifts. Sometimes our ambitions overreach our physical strength; we are called to bring them into harmony again. We would like to be perfect parents, excellent employees, generous parishioners, but we find that in the process we become instead exhausted, impatient with our children, and resentful of the demands placed on us. Asceticism means the acceptance of our limits and the search for a better balance. This is the kind of asceticism that is hardest for those who would be perfect in all respects, because it requires a painful letting go.

We practice asceticism in another way when we control our addictions, seek help for them, and recognize how we are using drugs, alcohol, or food in destructive ways. An addictive society such as ours witnesses to a variation on the traditional split between the spiritual and the material. Choked with material goods, our spirits are unable to breathe. What we really long for is genuine love and intimacy and some sense of purpose. Material goods will never give us these things.

Looking beyond our individual needs, there is an asceticism born of compassion which calls us to limit the consumerism into which we slip so that others may survive and thrive. It stems not from a desire to impose suffering on ourselves, as the old asceticism sometimes did, but from a capacity to hear the suffering of others and alleviate it. This asceticism expresses itself in care for the earth, restraint in our consumption, the foregoing of luxuries so that others can enjoy basic necessities. It stems not from the denial of the body in the classical sense, but from concern for the bodily integrity of those in need and awareness of the larger body of the world. It is an asceticism born of love and belief in the interconnectedness of all being.

Such compassionate asceticism is further expressed in action for justice. Dorothy Day describes it in terms of enduring the darkness, desolation, and inactivity of the prison cell where she was confined after picketing for the rights of political prisoners. Archbishop Oscar Romero conveys it in many of the statements he made before his assassination while saying Mass in March of 1980. Romero saw the poor as the body of Christ, and his persecution as the result of sharing in their destiny. He resolved to give his life for those he loved. Both Day and Romero reveal a kind of asceticism that is rooted in identification with the suffering of others. In a paradoxical way, Romero's courage in face of the opposition and threats on his life, circumstances that might be expected to produce fear and anxiety, inspired a physical serenity and energy he had not experienced before. Biographers report that before Romero's appointment as Archbishop of San Salvador and his commitment to the poor of his country, he suffered from weakness and nervous tension, finding it necessary to take periodic times out for rest. When he committed himself more deeply to the struggles of the poor, his physical strength increased.[3]

A healthy asceticism is the basis of creativity. Artists know that discipline frees their creative powers. The sudden flashes of discovery which occur in the process of creation are usually preceded by intense wrestling with problems. Wordsworth remarked that no valuable poems were produced except by one who had "thought long and deeply." Picasso's sketches for "Guernica," which show how he experimented with variations of meaning by trying different relations among the characters, are one example of the process of conscious and unconscious observing, sifting and shaping involved in creation. Inherent in the creative process is the discipline of developing the materials and skills which are the media for expressing ourselves creatively. The musician must learn the initial five-finger exercises; the calligrapher must get the basic forms.

A similar relationship between freedom and discipline exists in the spiritual life. Discipline is not meant to be a denial of our bodiliness;

rather, it frees us for the action of God in our lives. Though contemporary spirituality has rejected approaches to discipline and asceticism which imply a rejection of the body or the goodness of creation, it retains the conviction that a certain silence and discipline enable us to maintain our identity and spiritual freedom. Since human powers tend to dispersion or diffusion, it is necessary to center our energies, to form a contemplative body and mind. Such discipline applies to both body and spirit. Excessive amounts of food and drink can block one's creative powers, but so can inner turmoil, unresolved hurts, and anxiety about success or failure. In spiritual disciplines, as in artistic creation, setting certain boundaries allows creative energies to come to expression. We open ourselves to God, the deepest levels of the self, and all of creation when we impose on ourselves a moderate, purposeful discipline.

Notes

1. For an appreciation of the relationship between sexuality and spirituality, see James B. Nelson, *Embodiment: An Approach to Sexuality and Christian Theology* (Minneapolis: Augsburg Publishing Co., 1978); and Evelyn Eaton and James D. Whitehead, *A Sense of Sexuality. Christian Love and Intimacy* (New York: Doubleday & Co., 1989).

2. (Boston: Little, Brown & Co., 1963).

3. See James R. Brockman, *The Word Remains: A Life of Oscar Romero* (Maryknoll, NY: Orbis Books, 1982).

8

Work as Co-Creation

In *The Man Who Planted Trees* the French writer Jean Giono tells the story of Elzeard Bouffier, a farmer and shepherd who lives in a devastated section of southeastern France. Bouffier responds to this desolation in his native region of Provence by planting trees. For thirty years, while the rest of Europe is enveloped in two world wars, Bouffier daily places one hundred acorns in earth that has for generations been devoid of any living thing. He continues until he is well into his eighties, reaching an ever-broadening expanse of Provence. In time, waters that once swept away soil return to their rivulets. Plants revive. Animals return. Giono describes the transformation.

> Everything was changed. Even the air. Instead of the harsh dry winds that used to attack me, a gentle breeze was blowing, laden with scents. A sound like water came from the mountains: it was the wind in the forest. Most amazing of all, I heard the actual sound of water falling into a pool. I saw that a fountain had been built, that it flowed freely and—what touched me most—that someone had planted a linden beside it, a linden that must have been four years old, already in full leaf, the incontestable symbol of resurrection.[1]

The mysterious regeneration of the valleys and villages restores hope to the people who come there to live.

Giono's story is a parable of the combination of personal integrity and communal service many people long to realize in their work. Work is one of the most important ways in which we are related to all others in our world. We rely on the work of others to fill our most basic needs for food, shelter, and health; we meet the needs of others through our work. It is a human activity that calls out for a mutual rhythm of giving and receiving, learning and teaching. Those without work, the unemployed and the retired, feel like outsiders cut off from the ebb and flow of human life. Work is meant to be a communal experience, expressing our essential interrelatedness.

Our actual experience of work often falls short of this ideal. It may be marked by boredom, conflict, and competition rather than cooperation and creativity. Yet the greater number of our adult years are spent in some kind of work. Work is therefore a key dimension of our spirituality, influencing in many ways our experience of self, others, and God. Work can deaden and destroy us, or it can give expression to our strongest convictions and gifts. We will look first at the reasons why work is alienating for many people, then at its potential to become an experience of co-creation, and finally consider some practical ways of bringing about change in our work experience.

Alienating Work

Many of us do not like our work. We find it hard, meaningless, life-draining. It is not large enough for us, and constricts rather than expands our spirits. We want a vocation, not just a job. Even among those of us who enjoy our work, questions remain. The world of work calls for efficiency, competition, profit. We cannot see how it relates to the Christian emphasis on love, community and compassion. As one woman said, "I want to know how you can make it in the work world and still remain a Christian."

We often find the experience of work to be one of alienation. This alienation takes many forms: mind from body, activity from our deepest self, worker from worker. Work then leads to individual and social illness. We feel devalued and our gifts unappreciated. We produce goods and services that are consumed and have no lasting existence; we are not even certain of their quality or value. We see only one small part of the totality and find no connection between the job we perform and the larger whole. The sale of a product, for example, leaves no necessary connection between two people. I can go into a furniture store, pay the salesperson for a lamp and walk out. I may never see her again. In fact this disconnectedness is often considered a value in the world of commerce. We don't want to be bothered by stories from a clerk's personal life. They may annoy us and cause us to shop elsewhere.

Alienation can also result from not really knowing what we are producing—whether these are products that heal or weapons of death. In the course of our work we are asked to take actions that separate us from our own humanity and that of others. No purpose is apparent beyond the doing of a job. Furthermore, work is restricted to paid work; what goes without financial reward is devalued, and work itself is evaluated on the basis of the financial rewards it provides. Important work such as caring for and nurturing children, or creating works of art that expand the human spirit, go unregarded. Work is valued for the material goods it can procure, not for its own intrinsic worth. It is but a means to an end. Sometimes we endure it for that reason, using up most of our years in the process. On a larger scale, the works we create take on lives of their own and come to dominate our lives. Nuclear weapons are but the most potent example of this. Alienated work affects the whole fiber of individual and society.

This problem is intensified in Third World countries where the majority of the population labors long hours for wages that cannot support even a minimum level of human existence. Women, especially, bear this burden of exhausting work that kills the body and spirit. Some of the elements of this alienation were described by the French philosopher and mystic, Simone Weil. Weil entered the factory system herself for a year and experienced first-hand the way labor often forces us to sacrifice human values and expectations in order to earn a livelihood. Work in these settings diminishes the self and increases our sense of powerlessness. Often it violates standards of health and well-being, dividing people from one another by the anonymity of assembly lines or the drive of competition. Much of women's labor, which produces over fifty percent of the Third

World's food, is invisible. After a full day of paid labor, these women face a heavy schedule of work at home.

Clearly work in our world is in need of redemption, and is a major area of concern for any contemporary spirituality. To bring about change in this area, we must begin to imagine together. The individual imagination can soon reach the limits of its power. It is difficult for individuals to keep alive hopeful images of the future or to tell a story that has a happy ending. Negative images can shock us into action—but only if they are accompanied by positive images. These positive images not only show us a new future; they help to produce the energy which brings it about.

Work As Co-Creation

Some years ago, in *The Divine Milieu,* Teilhard de Chardin focused on the religious meaning of human action.[2] He noted that many people spend most of their lives at work, yet see no connection between that work and the reality of God in their lives. He urged us to try to see the connection, even the physical connection, between our work and the coming of the reign of God. Teilhard was convinced that everything could contribute to that end and therefore have intrinsic value.

An image that has been used recently to describe our relationship to God's creative activity can provide the basis for such a spirituality of work. This is the metaphor of co-creation.[3] To speak of co-creation is to affirm that creation is not a once-and-for-all static act. The world is in process; it is ever being formed. Therefore we should not speak of creation only in the past tense, of God having created the world. The creative process did not end with the six days of intense divine activity recorded in Genesis. We speak, rather, of the world as being created even now, as continually coming into existence. Chaos and nothingness are not something that happened once upon a time in the past; they are constant threats to life.

Co-creation means dealing with the void within us and the potential destruction outside of us. God accompanies the human race through its history. We are made in the divine image and entrusted with responsibility for the ongoing movement of creation. The image of co-creation grounds our own creativity and enables us to share in God's creativity and concern for the future of the world.

In the book of Genesis, work is at first described as painless and integral to life. Before the fall, tilling and keeping the garden, the biblical expressions for human work, are connoted with pleasure and joy. This labor is an expression of human dignity and integrity, an experience of participation which requires care and attention. Expulsion from the garden symbolizes the rupture that occurs, and work afterwards shares in the history of alienation. This is the basis of the tradition that views work as a curse accompanied by hardship and difficulty.

Redemption is the ongoing healing of our world which we, with God, work at together. This is the deeper meaning of solidarity and co-creation. The biblical model of redemption is that of reconciliation, the reordering of relationships within the whole body. Co-creation thus becomes a form of healing. The vision of reconciliation affirms God's desire for relatedness in creation. Our work is cooperative or co-creative with divine creativity, co-redemptive with divine redemption.

Some fear that this notion of co-creation will lessen the power of God. This is to view creativity as a limited substance to be divided up between God and humans, and so to distort its meaning. Rather, God creates to a great extent through us, and the more we develop our creativity, the more we further the purposes of God. Creativity is basic to everything, both divine and human. As the Genesis story tells us, God's creativity is boundless; all things depend on this divine creative action.

As a redemptive activity, work enables us to participate in the coming of the reign of God. If we are to share in creative activity with God, we must have some idea of God's purpose. What we are striving for in all our work is what the Hebrew scriptures describe as *shalom*.[4] We have usually translated this Hebrew word as *peace*, but its meaning is much larger than what we usually think of as peace. The Hebrew scriptures use the term *shalom* to denote the right ordering of all things according to God's purpose, that harmony which reaches from an individual's heart to relations between persons and nations and to all of creation. This *shalom* begins and ends in the heart of God, but it encompasses all areas of life. All human work has this eschatological fullness for its goal and is judged by the call to live in justice, which it implies.

Jesus' message of the reign of God tells us that we participate in the work of creation when we undo evil, when we alleviate human suffering and strive for justice in the world. In preaching the reign of God Jesus offered a future to a people caught in the grim reality of their present.

> The blind receive their sight,
> the lame walk,
> lepers are cleansed,
> the deaf hear,
> the dead are raised up,
> and the poor have good news preached to them. (Lk 7:22)

Jesus announces possibilities that have been defined as impossibilities. The truth of the reign of God can only be grasped by the imagination; it begins in poetry. For it is the truth of paradox: "To find your life you must lose it." "The last shall be first." "When I am weak, I am strong." These are statements whose terms contradict one another; they express mysteries which cannot be captured in logical categories. Keeping the Christian paradox alive means believing in life when there are many reasons to despair.

How does this translate into the life of an aerospace engineer, a department store sales clerk, a receptionist in a dental office? These jobs can seem quite mundane, not only some distance from the reign of God but at times actually contradicting and compromising its values. The challenge is to learn to find ways of living out discipleship in our ordinary work settings. How do Jesus' words about the reign of God intersect with what we do in our jobs each day? One young woman answered this question by recalling what her mother, Genevieve, had taught her. Genevieve was on the housekeeping staff of a large city hospital, and she went about her job each day with a sense that she was contributing to a larger healing process. Patients and staff knew her by name and loved her. Genevieve was the one some patients stopped to tell of their fears or victories. Her faith told her, she said, that following Jesus meant restoring dignity and hope to people's lives. Business executives, lawyers, teachers, receptionists—any occupation provides opportunities for giving control of people's lives back to them, for reducing some of the circumstances that dehumanize persons in our culture. In our last section we will look further at some practical implications of seeing human work as directed to re-creating the world.

Changing Our Experience of Work

If work is to be co-creation with God, then the changes we make in our experience of work will flow from the following convictions:

1) *Work should be an expression of our centered selves, the source of our originality and creativity.* Sometimes it takes many years to discover that true self. Searching for it takes the same path as that of contemplation, what has been called bringing the mind into the heart. It is the process by which we discover the deepest levels of our creativity and thereby learn what it is that we love to do. That is why the basis of discernment is the effort to find our true self, our center. This is the root of choice. It is here, at our true center, that we find our truth, talent, originality, energy, and courage. In other words, it is here that we discover our call and vocation.

2) *Work should not only engage our individual gifts; it should contribute to the healing of society.* A key question as I evaluate my work choices is: Among all the things I could do, what would most contribute to the reign of God, to the kind of world Jesus described and labored to bring about? Consideration of this question may result in a choice to remain in centers of political and economic power in order to change systems at that level. It may lead to a new recognition of ways in which my present work could contribute more to societal well-being. It may mean preferring work which does more good for others to work which brings me greater financial returns.

We need the courage to change work when it does not bring us happiness or provide us with a sense of purpose. Our vocational identity develops over time. Questions of call and work are never answered once and for all, but must be asked anew at various points in our lives. One off-shoot of today's emphasis on process is that we can go through several work experiences in the course of a lifetime. Our choices need to be constantly evaluated. Sometimes there are financial contraints on our ability to change our work. We have few choices if we are a single parent supporting children or have no skill level that enables us to transfer to another job. But there are times when we stay with work long after we feel dissatisfied, because we have not the courage to change.

Often we know that we could be happier with fewer material objects than we have, that what we most long for is a deeper sense of purpose and integrity. For example, a newly-married couple choose to share a home with another family with five children. This enables them to cut expenses enough to work for a lesser-paying recycling firm. A physicist leaves a job in a research institute because she can no longer work with integrity in that place. She makes much less money but finds more peace in making it. An artist chooses to live simply in order to touch the human spirit through his paintings.

The parable of the rich young man raises this question in a poignant way. What should I do to be saved, the man asks? In other words, how can I heal my life from its boredom and fragmentation? He is aware that something is lacking in his life. He has many material possessions, but they do not give him what he wants. Jesus offers him a kind of poverty that would be fullness, but he turns away from it. We must keep alive this gospel challenge as we choose how we will use our talents in the public world of work.

3) *Prayer is an important aspect of the work of co-creativity.* It empowers us to relinquish the fears and desires which obstruct the play of God's creativity, and enables God's transformation to operate more freely and powerfully in us and those connected with us. Prayer as a conscious orientation to God enables us to image God's purposes with greater fidelity, and to unite intentionally with the divine creativity so as to become a more potent force in the creation of a more beautiful world.

Prayer and action are a question of the inner and outer work in us. They are interdependent. Frequently we fail to hear the anger, pain, joy, or fear in ourselves and see its connection with what is happening in our work. Prayer forces us to listen to it honestly. It also requires leisure. In ancient times a seventh part of a person's time—Sunday and the sabbatical or seventh year—were set aside for non-work. Today if a person gets a sabbatical, it is usually considered a chance to catch up on the unfinished work of the previous six years. However, in numerology the number seven stands for ripening or fullness. Leisure allows time for the ripening and coming to fullness of the inner life.

4) *We need to be attentive to opportunities for renewal right within our work itself.* Often in the course of our work there are brief glimpses of mystery that refresh. We are privileged to share in moments of human suffering and healing, in struggles with hardship and breakthroughs into victory. We are given the gift of entering into the depths of the human and are healed as well. We experience the grace in the lives of ordinary women and men, and are transformed by the experience. Once when I asked a young woman to choose a symbol for God, she immediately thought of the face of Susan, a developmentally disabled adult with whom she worked at a group home. "Yes," she said, "God is reflected in the faces of these people I work with." Finding God requires an attentive and open spirit, but those who can look at times on the face of mystery find that their work satisfies and renews them even though it may not make them wealthy.

Jacob Needleman describes this experience of mystery within one's work in *The Way of the Physician.*[5] In the midst of new medical technologies and the specter of malpractice, Needleman calls upon doctors to return once again to their original vocation. Needleman constructs his book as a series of letters to his boyhood physician, whom he remembers as a great doctor. His prescription for healing the malaise of alienation and boredom which ails modern medicine is to call physicians to a search for truth. This will lead to once again connecting with the sources of healing energy derived from a higher source, and becoming a channel of that energy for others. Needleman wants to rekindle in the medical profession a sense of moral wonder that will enable the physician in each moment to see the world and each patient anew. The meaning of being a physician can only be found again, Needleman believes, through recovery of the question of the meaning of human life itself.

5) *Attempts to improve our work environments are an important expression of Christian love.* If liberated work is to be more than an impossible dream, it will require changing the quality of working life. We must care about and seek to eliminate such problems as chemical hazards that affect health, inequities in pay scales, sexual harassment on the job, noise pollution and poor ventilation, and the subordination of people to demands for high output. We need to struggle for good child care, flexible schedules, and styles of management that put people rather than unlimited competition and productivity at the the center of planning. These may seem like small issues, but when we free individual gifts, care for workers' spirits and bodies, and create community in the workplace, we promote social justice in an immediate and tangible way.

The world of work is especially difficult to tackle. So many powerful forces are responsible for the patterns that now exist. Yet even here surprising things can happen. Jesus tells us a story of just such an unexpected shift in perspectives. It is the account of the workers in the vineyard (Mt 20:1-16). The usual arguments about what is fitting or possible are less important than the message of God's graciousness that cuts across them. The story presents two ways of regarding our worth: grace and merit. The logic of merit views the world of work in everyday terms—we labor and receive what we deserve. But a logic of grace moves through these expectations, asking us to view life in a surprising way. The behavior of the vineyard owner is not what we would expect under the circumstances. In the story we are confronted by Jesus' vision of reality, a vision which contradicts human ambitions. The parable calls for a thorough reorientation of our values and attitudes. The world of work today calls for a similar revamping, a movement from work as primarily a means to economic security and consumption; a movement from aggressive competitiveness, hierarchical management models, and a win-lose decision-making style; a movement from work that separates human beings from one another and from the earth.

We began this chapter with the story of a man who planted trees, the story of an individual whose work brought personal satisfaction and happiness and at the same time contributed to the renewal of public life. Someone has suggested that there is a new, global metaphor which can draw us together: trees. A Los Angeles environmental group, Tree People, backed by the American Forestry Association, took action in 1988 to counteract global warming. They began planting trees. In yards. Along city streets. In the countryside. Trees absorb the carbon dioxide which produces the unwanted greenhouse effect. The Tree People point to other benefits of their work. Tree plantings draw people together, show them how to live harmoniously with nature, and create community where it did not exist before. All these are the values we hope for in a new approach to work. Perhaps tree planting is a good metaphor for human work as well.

Notes

1.   (Vermont: Chelsea Green Publishing Co., 1985), p. 34.

2.   (New York: Harper & Row Publishers, 1960), pp. 64-67.

3.   Dorothy Soelle explores the relationship between human work and divine creation in *To Work and To Love. A Theology of Creation* (Philadelphia: Fortress Press, 1984). See also Joe Holland, *Creative Communion: Toward a Spirituality of Work* (Mahwah, New Jersey: Paulist Press, 1989).

4.   Walter Brueggemann discusses the many meanings of *shalom* in *Living Toward a Vision: Biblical Reflection on Shalom* (Philadelphia: United Church Press, 1982).

5.   (San Francisco: Harper & Row, 1985).

9

Mending the Connections

In the opening section of her book on family ritual and community celebration, *To Dance With God,* Gertrud Nelson tells a story about her three-year-old daughter, Annika. Gertrude had been sewing one afternoon, filling the wastebasket near her sewing machine with scraps of fabric. Annika, fascinated by the discards, searched through them for long bright strips and carried them off. When Gertrude paused to check on her daughter, she found her sitting in the grass in the back yard with a long pole. She was taping the scraps to the top of the pole. "I'm making a banner for a procession," she said. "I need a procession so that God will come down and dance with us." Annika then lifted her banner to the wind and began to dance.[1]

This child's play reminds us that the mending of creation, the recovery of our connections with God and all of creation, is not achieved by reason and will alone. The word salvation, from the root *salvus,* means healed. This healing reaches us especially through those channels that are able to touch body, mind, and spirit. It is ritual and celebration that keep wonder, renewal, an appreciation of beauty, and a capacity for joy alive among us. Such a spirit of celebration, whether found in a neighborhood softball game, an evening of laughter with friends, or a eucharistic celebration within a community of faith, is a vital part of the spiritual journey.

In this last chapter we will reflect on the crucial role played by the imagination and ritual in our spiritual lives. They are key agents in bringing about the change of heart this book envisions.

Spirituality and the Imagination

One of the things I remember most vividly from my Roman Catholic childhood is the celebration of feasts and the fulfillment of traditional rituals. They provided me with a sense of the rhythm of the seasons; the experience of being rooted in a wider community; some answers to questions about who I was and what was expected of me; and an opportunity to express feelings of longing, hope, guilt, and gratitude. I recall very little of the doctrine I must have learned during those years. But I do retain memories of the feelings of expectation engendered in me as we lighted the Advent wreath; images of solemnly receiving ashes on Ash Wednesday, making the stations of the cross during Lent; memories of holding palm branches on Palm Sunday, observing the three hours of silence on Good Friday, welcoming Easter with a sense of new energy and life; and images of crowning the statue of Mary amid the strong fragrance of fresh May lilacs. These were sensuous, bodily experiences which stimulated my imagination.

If we seek to mend broken connections we must appeal to the imagination.[2] The imagination is often thought to be the realm of children and fantasy; we equate it with the unreal and the unreliable. But in fact it is on the level of the imagination that we know and experience *reality* in its wholeness and connections. Through the imagination we know not simply the problem of homelessness, but this old alcoholic man sleeping on the streets of our city; not just the idea of community, but these people I live with who sometimes delight and at other times exasperate me. Reason abstracts from these connections to make general statements about life; the imagination knows concepts and information, but it knows them in the living color of their original settings.

The imagination expresses itself in myth and story, symbol and ritual, art and poetry. All of them give us compelling images. We tell stories or myths about who we are, where we have come from, where we are going and how we should live. The word myth is sometimes used to describe what we doubt to be true; however, in its original meaning, a myth is a story that is profoundly true in what it seeks to convey, even if its terms are not to be taken literally. Myth is a celebration of our central values. We take on the qualities of our myths, whether the myth be the story of Adam and Eve in Genesis or the more contemporary American myth of progress.

Telling stories is the best way to bring God's love to life in the community of faith. Remembering is a collective activity that unites us. It reclarifies our identity and gives a certain form to the bonds that unite us. The Book of Deuteronomy warns that if a community forgets its story of God and its common heritage, it will cease to be a people: "Be sure that if you forget your God . . . . you will most certainly perish" (Dt 8:19).

Our lives of faith are interwoven with those of our foremothers and forefathers and of future generations.

> What we have heard and known for ourselves,
> and what ancestors have told us,
> must not be withheld from their descendants,
> but handed on by us to the next generation,
> that is: the titles of God, the divine power
> and the miracles God has done (Ps 78:3-4).

Remembering is an act of hope that unites the past, present and future of a community. In the Jewish Passover liturgy, the head of the household not only explains the special features of the meal and proclaims the essentials of the story, but also looks forward to redemption in the future (Ex 12:26). The messiah will inaugurate a new community for all peoples, when sorrow and death are things of the past (Is 25:6-8; 65:11-13; Zeph 1:7). The condition of death from which we need deliverance is one in which personal relationships to God and others have been forgotten, the condition of the land of forgetfulness (Ps 88:11-12).

A family, like a community, has stories and rituals that create an atmosphere of belonging and sharing. Through ritual we receive and pass along the collective treasures we call tradition. Each story and ceremony tells us that we are parts of a whole. Their purpose is to integrate us as individuals into a community. Through ritual we capture at least momentarily that deep intuition we have of a real and spiritual unity in all things. We overcome, if only briefly, the human divisions and conditions that separate human beings and set us at odds with nature. Reflection on the Christian celebration of the Eucharist enables us to understand this more fully.

Eucharist and the Collective Imagination

The apostle Paul, writing to Christian Corinth about AD 56, recalls the command of Jesus, "Do this in memory of me." The Eucharist is a statement that we live in three-dimensional time, between past and future, between the coming of Jesus and the final establishment of the reign of God. In it we remember that "God has raised Jesus from the dead and therefore all those who believe in him." Thus Eucharist is a memorial which inspires us to do what we can, and a prophecy that inspires us to attempt what appears impossible. It stands in judgment on our present reality.

Liturgy is many things, but one of its most powerful dimensions is its expression of connection. It binds us to the past, to creation, and to one another. Ritual catches up past events and provides us with a sense of continuity. In the Eucharist we repeat Jesus' words, "Do this in memory of me." Memory is not simply a recalling of past events. In it we become aware of our links with the past. In addition, the symbols of the liturgy remind us that nature is being transformed as we are. In fact, that our transformation depends on that of nature. Through all of the sacraments we implicitly express our love for and reliance on the earth. We use symbols in our rituals, universal symbols such as light, fire, water, bread, and wine. They are rich with the levels of meaning of body, grain, harvest, yeast, vineyards. Each celebration of them must then be a commitment to preserving these gifts which bring God to us. If we do not care for creation, there will be no bread and wine for our Eucharist.

Symbol revives our sense of the wonder in the ordinary. A vivid statement of this occurs in Thornton Wilder's play, *Our Town*, which focuses on the value of the smallest aspects of our daily lives.[3] After Emily, one of the play's main characters, has died in childbirth, Wilder has her ask the Stage Manager if she can return home to relive just one day. The Stage

Manager warns that it isn't wise, but reluctantly agrees. Emily chooses to return on her twelfth birthday. She is deeply affected by the beauty of the ordinary and our lack of awareness of it—clocks ticking, sunflowers, food and coffee, new-ironed dresses and hot baths, sleeping and waking up. She cries out that earth is too wonderful for anybody to ever realize it. Then she asks the Stage Manager if any human beings ever realize life while they live it. "No," he says. And then, after pausing, adds: "The saints and poets, maybe—they do some." Liturgy exists to alert us to the wonder of creation.

All of nature, not just the human, discloses the divine mystery. Nature is God's embodiment, making visible the presence and love of God. Many biblical texts witness to this sacramentality of nature. One that is striking is the section of the Book of Job in which God recounts to Job the marvelous wonders of creation.

> Has the rain a father?
>   Who begets the dewdrops?
> What womb brings forth the ice,
>   and gives birth to the frost of heaven,
> when the waters grow hard as stone
>   and the surface of the deep congeals? (38:28-30)

Job replies:

> I had heard of you by word of mouth,
>   but now my eye has seen you" (42:5).

Such passages call us to see nature as a bestower of grace, enabling us to find within nature the divine and creative Wisdom which was God's "delight day by day, playing before God all the while, playing on the surface of the earth" (Pr 8:30-31).

In the Eucharistic liturgy, the preface includes the phrase, "All creation gives you praise." One Lutheran version reads: "You have filled all creation with light and life: everything everywhere is full of your glory." These prayers convey the fact that the Eucharist is introducing us to a new vision of all creation. The Eucharist is not only a confirmation of our solidarity, as members of Christ's body, with the rest of humanity; it is a confirmation of our solidarity with the rest of creation, including the earth. The bread and wine gathered from the scattered hills remind us not only of the gathering of people, but of the earth—apart from whose wholeness the human community cannot experience its own wholeness.

Liturgy is about the healing of relationships. During his ministry Jesus shared many meals with diverse groups of people. The gospels describe meals eaten with the poor, the rich, the uneducated, the learned, the powerless and the powerful. All of these meals were leavened by Jesus' presence. All of them brought people together. Sharing in food was the expression of a much broader and deeper sharing.

In the Eucharist we acknowledge our hunger and share food given us as gift to satisfy that hunger. This meal cannot be celebrated honestly if we ignore the hungers of the world and our call to share food on a broader plane. It is an action meant to be paradigmatic of our actions in the rest of life. Jesus' celebration of his Last Supper with his disciples revealed a new solidarity that moved beyond family. It showed us that all people could exist as brothers and sisters and share the earth's resources. The Eucharist is about life on all levels; in it we are committed to bringing life to others as Jesus did—at the level of their need, whatever that may be.

The gospel accounts make clear the connection between discipleship and feeding the hungry. In John's accounts of the feeding of the 5000, and in the response of the Risen Jesus to Peter, this language of food and feeding recurs as the commission of discipleship. We are apt to hear it only on a symbolic level, thinking mainly of people's spiritual needs. However, the New Testament does not allow this. In the letter to the Corinthians which Paul wrote in about 56 BCE, he expresses his shock at the way the agape meal or sharing of food was occurring before the celebration of the Lord's Supper.

> First of all: I hear that when you gather for a meeting there are divisions among you, and I am inclined to believe it (1 Cor 11:18).

Groups of people were celebrating a common meal before the Lord's Supper, and doing so according to their social and economic status. Wealthy Christians shared sumptuous feasts with their wealthy friends. The differences in the way the rich and poor ate stood out in glaring fashion:

> When you assemble it is not to eat the Lord's Supper, for everyone is in haste to eat their own supper. One person is hungry while another gets drunk. . . . Would you show such contempt for the Church of God and embarrass those who have nothing? (1 Cor 11:20-22)

Paul recognizes the threat such divisions pose for any community. These actions, he warns the Corinthians, contradict the meaning of the Eucharist, for Paul emphasizes that in breaking the bread participants become one body. Those who eat Christ's body are interdependent, bearing responsibility for the poor and needy. A community celebration of the Eucharist commits Christians to struggle against everything that harms the body of Christ.

Recent liturgical changes in the Catholic Church have enriched all the sacraments with rites that reinforce their communitarian dimension. Eucharist is a restorative sacrament for those who struggle day after day with injustices. It is a sign that one day the reign will be more manifest than often appears to be possible.

Ritual and Remembering in Life Passages

What is true of Eucharist is also true of the other Christian sacraments. These community celebrations renew and sustain us at important times of transition. During transitions the connections in our lives are especially at risk. Transitions are experiences of vulnerability when we must embrace the new without losing either our identity or our hope: birth/initiation, puberty, leaving home, marriage, loss and sickness, retirement, death. We sense that we are in danger, at risk during these passages. It is then that we need especially to remember the death and resurrection of Jesus, the passage par excellence.   The sacraments aid us by bringing this paschal mystery to bear on our life passages.

In addition to the official sacraments which are part of our religious traditions, we need other rituals.   The sacraments are meant to be paradigms or patterns of what happens in all of life. We nourish our spiritual lives not only by keeping alive traditional rituals, but by creating new ones. Marie Fortune, in *Sexual Violence. The Unmentionable Sin*, describes the significance such a ritual has for healing.

> A woman who had been raped realized that she felt somehow stained by the assault. It was not that she felt dirty or stigmatized by the sexual contact per se. Rather, in the violation of her person, she felt that something had been put on her which she could not cast off. So she decided that she wanted to experience some form of ritual cleansing in order to be cleansed of the violation. She sought the help of a woman minister friend who suggested that she gather her close friends and then use water to wash away the stain of violation.[4]

This way of bringing healing renews the woman's conviction that she is not alone in her experience.

A group of students in a course I taught on ministry with the aging developed several such rituals.   One young man said that his father had been quite depressed since his retirement, and the son realized that the family had never done anything special to mark that event. He called for a supper celebration to which each family member brought two symbols: a symbol of something they were grateful for that was a fruit of the father's working years, and a symbol of a hope they had for his future. One son, who found it hard to talk to his dad, brought his college diploma, and, supported by the symbol, was able to thank his dad for paying for his education.

Another woman student developed a ritual for the event of her mother's move from the family home of forty years to an apartment. All of the family who could come gathered at the home. They moved from room to room of the sprawling house, pausing in each to tell stories and remember special times that had hallowed each room. Then they recited a psalm and gave their mother a symbol of that space—pictures, a vase, a pillow—to accompany her to her new apartment, reminders that she was not leaving behind the years in that house, but taking them with her. The ritual concluded with a champagne celebration in the living room. Both rituals reveal the power of the imagination to open us to new possibilities in events.

Like the seven sacraments, these other rituals reinsert us into the web of existence with hope. Birthday parties are a reminder that life is a gift from the first moment, and that it continues to be given to us through our friendships. That is why we celebrate birthdays with a community of friends. When someone is ill or a family faces a crisis, we bring flowers, bake food, and send messages of support; we are reminded of the social nature of sickness and healing. In our work for social justice, we pause to acknowledge and give thanks for our partial successes—a new housing project for the homeless, a woman starting a new life after wife battering— and by doing so we nourish the springs of our hope and energy.

When ritual and celebration decline in our lives, so does a sense of our connections. The experience of joy goes as well. Sometimes the nameless nostalgia we feel around feasts such as Christmas or Thanksgiving reveals a longing for the kind of bonds that traditions supply. Because traditions point to the past they include all who have gone before us. A ritual that is old and rich in meaning gathers up all the fruits of the imagination that have been expended on it. The seasons of the liturgical year enable us to enter into the various facets of the gift of God as we move from Advent to Epiphany, from Lent to Easter and Pentecost.

Through ritual and celebration we speak the language of the imagination. It is no accident that our preoccupation with the isolated individual has developed during a period when reason has been considered the most reliable way to truth. Reason abstracts and isolates. The inability to connect is one symptom of the loss of the imagination in our time; recovery of the imagination remains one of the best ways to restore community and compassion to our lives.

We began our reflections on contemporary spirituality by exploring our current world view. It is in light of this story or world view that we answer such questions as, What is the nature of reality? How are we a part of it? How shall we describe God and others and our relationship to them? Although the prevailing world view influences our answers to life's most fundamental questions, that world view itself is often so much a part of our lives that we fail to notice it. It is made up of assumptions that permeate and sustain daily life, like the air we breathe.

In view of the massive global threats to life in our time, it is urgent that we recognize and revise our assumptions, that we take responsibility for how we are naming reality as we move into the next century. If we refuse to do so, we will forfeit the future. We must share God's concern for this world, and reclaim all those connections that have been lost in a fragmented universe. A renewed spirituality will help us reestablish these connections. It must be a holistic spirituality in which realities such as work and prayer, body and spirit, nature and humanity will each find a place of honor within one dynamic and interdependent whole.

Notes

1. (Mahwah, New Jersey: Paulist Press, 1986), p. 3.
2. For further reflection on the importance of the imagination for spirituality, see Kathleen Fischer, *The Inner Rainbow: The Imagination in Christian Life* (New York: Paulist Press, 1983).
3. (New York: Harper & Row, 1957).
4. (New York: The Pilgrim Press, 1983), p. 222.

For Further Reading

Boyer, Ernest. *A Way in the World; Family Life As Spiritual Discipline.* San Francisco: Harper & Row, 1984.

Brown, Robert McAfee. *Spirituality and Liberation: Overcoming the Great Fallacy.* Philadelphia: Westminster, 1988.

Carmody, John. *Ecology and Religion: Toward a New Christian Theology of Nature.* New York: Paulist, 1983.

Casey, Julian. *Where Is God Now? Nuclear Terror, Feminism and the Search for God.* Kansas City: Sheed & Ward, 1987.

Conn, Joann Wolski, ed. *Women's Spirituality: Resources for Christian Development.* New Jersey: Paulist, 1987.

Edwards, Tilden H., ed. *Living With Apocalypse: Spiritual Resources for Social Compassion.* New York: Harper & Row, 1984.

Fox, Matthew. *The Coming of the Cosmic Christ.* San Francisco: Harper & Row, 1988.

Grassi, J. A. *Broken Bread and Broken Bodies: The Lord's Supper and World Hunger.* Maryknoll, NY: Orbis Books, 1985.

Gutierrez, Gustavo. *We Drink From Our Own Wells.: The Spiritual Journey of a People.* Maryknoll, NY: Orbis Books, 1984.

Jäger, Willigis. *The Way to Contemplation: Encountering God Today.* New Jersey: Paulist Press, 1987.

Lee, Bernard J. and Michael A. Cowan. *Dangerous Memories: House Churches and Our American Story.* Kansas City: Sheed & Ward, 1986.

Lonergan, Anne and Caroline Richards, ed. *Thomas Berry and the New Cosmology.* Mystic, CT: Twenty-Third Publications, 1987.

May, Gerald. *Addiction and Grace.* San Francisco: Harper & Row, 1988.

Mollenkott, Virginia. *Godding: Human Responsibility and the Bible.* New York: Crossroad, 1987.

Perlinski, Jerome, ed. *The Spirit of the Earth: A Teilhard Centennial Celebration.* New York: Seabury, 1981.

Shannon, William H. *Seeking the Face of God.* New York: Crossroad, 1988.

Whitehead, Evelyn Eaton, and James D. *A Sense of Sexuality: Christian Love and Intimacy.* New York: Doubleday, 1989.